"If you're sitting down to write your first screenplay, you need to read this book. If you've written a couple of screenplays and are still trying to break in, you need to read this book. Hell, if you've been earning your living writing screenplays for the past six years, you should read this book. Informative, provocative, illustrative — all the qualities of the great teacher Tom Lazarus are right here. Indispensable for anyone who writes or is thinking about writing movies."
> — Scott Frank, screenwriter: *Get Shorty, Out of Sight, Minority Report*

"Some of Hollywood's most successful writers whisper about learning it from Tom! His approach is unorthodox, but crystal clear and on the money. A master at teaching the elusive art of good screenwriting. *The Last Word* is his best book yet."
> — Sid Ganis, producer and past president of the Academy of Motion
> Picture Arts and Sciences

"Smart, funny, and helpful to the max. A cleverly organized book of tips for the professional and would-be professional. A stellar read. Recommended for every screenwriter's bookshelf."
> — Bonnie MacBird, screenwriter: *Tron*, Emmy-winning producer, and
> former Universal Studios feature film story exec

"Lazarus gets down to the nitty-gritty aspects of screenwriting that you don't find elsewhere, with sound advice on how to avoid the pitfalls of storytelling, using his signature humor and no-nonsense approach to lay out the last word in screenwriting."
> — Chrys Balis, screenwriter: *Asylum*, script consultant and writer for
> network and cable television

"The ultimate screenwriter's companion. Read it, reread it, enjoy it, learn from it and apply the information within. My highest recommendation."
> — Stefan Blitz, editor-in-chief, ForcesOfGeek.com

"Lazarus says 'grab the reader by the throat early on and never let go.' In *The Last Word*, Lazarus follows his own advice. He grabs the screenwriter by the throat and doesn't let go until the script works! Short, urgent, and useful. Real-world advice from a successful screenwriter.
> — Tony Levelle, author: *Digital Video Secrets* and *Producing with
> Passion*

"Tom Lazarus serves up non-nonsense story development notes in a clear, authoritative voice. He's the kind of ally smart writers want as they confront the blank page."
> — David McKenna, author: *Memo From the Story Department*

"A terrific guide for beginners."
— John Badham, director: *Saturday Night Fever, WarGames, Short Circuit*

"Golden nuggets along the Yellow Brick Road, which every screenwriter needs to heed. I will recommend this book to every one of my clients... but only if I get one first."
— Stan Williams, author: *The Moral Premise*

"Serves up a delicious feast of what all writers most need but seldom get — the truth. Want praise for every page you write? Ask Mom. Want to learn, grow, and become a top screenwriter? Take a deep breath and read *The Last Word*. It's an enormously practical, lucid, spot-on book that will make you a stronger writer."
— Eric Edson, screenwriter, professor, author of *The Story Solution: 23 Actions All Great Heroes Must Take*

"Reading this book is like having a writing coach in your ear, giving you helpful tips for creating your best work. A valuable resource for any storyteller."
— Tom Farr, blogger: A Journey of Faith and Creativity

"Takes screenwriting books to the next level. Think of this as going to grad school. Tom Lazarus has walked the halls of Hollywood in both film and television and knows how things work."
— D.B. Gilles, author: *The Screenwriter Within, 2nd Edition*

"Spells out the basics of screenwriting in a clear and concise way. Ignore the words of Mr. Lazarus at your peril. This book is simple, to the point, and invaluable."
— Matthew Terry, filmmaker/screenwriter/teacher, reviewer for Microfilmmaker.com

"A practical, A-to-Z overview of some of the most common storytelling roadblocks that can spell the difference between a 'pass' and a 'sale' in a competitive marketplace!"
— Kathie Fong Yoneda, consultant, workshop leader, author: *The Script-Selling Game: A Hollywood Insider's Look at Getting Your Script Sold and Produced*

"Really good advice delivered in a really practical way. Tom Lazarus shows you bad writing and improved writing, and the light bulb goes on. Seeing the mistakes other writers make gives insights into the writing process that you don't often find. It promotes letting go of that critical voice that says 'I'm no good at this' or 'Who does he think he is?' so you can take advantage of good feedback. This is a book I will keep on my bookshelf!"
— Kim Hudson, author: *The Virgin's Promise*

TOM LAZARUS

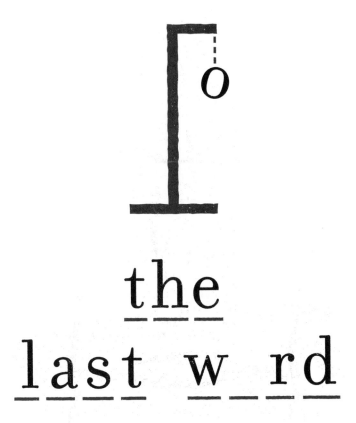

the
last w rd

DEFINITIVE ANSWERS TO ALL YOUR
screenwriting questions

MICHAEL WIESE PRODUCTIONS

Published by Michael Wiese Productions
12400 Ventura Blvd. #1111
Studio City, CA 91604
(818) 379-8799, (818) 986-3408 (FAX)
mw@mwp.com
www.mwp.com

Cover design by MWP
Interior design by William Morosi
Printed by McNaughton & Gunn

Manufactured in the United States of America
Copyright © 2012 by Tom Lazarus

Library of Congress Cataloging-in-Publication Data

Lazarus, Tom.
The last word : definitive answers to all your screenwriting questions / Tom Lazarus.
    p. cm.
ISBN 978-1-61593-119-4 (pbk.)
1. Motion picture authorship. I. Title.
PN1996.L375 2012
808.2'3--dc23
                                        2012016108

table of contents

introduction

Where the hell do I get off writing a book giving definitive answers to all your screenwriting questions?

Well, I've written more than fifty original screenplays, over a hundred hours of television, seven produced features, directed four films and thirty hours of television, written and directed documentaries, award-winning educational and business films, music videos, and I've read and critiqued countless scripts. I've published two books — one on screenwriting, the other on rewriting.

I've worked in motion picture marketing for Fox and Universal, Seven Arts, Avco-Embassy, and I wrote the original screenplay for the hit, *Stigmata*, the #1 movie in America upon its release.

I mentor screenwriters online and have worked with writers from Russia, Australia, Canada, Japan, France, Brazil, Mexico, England, and Kazakhstan.

Recently I wrote and directed a sold-out theatre piece and am writing a follow-up show.

For twenty years I've taught The Master Class in Screenwriting, Advanced Feature Film Writing and Advanced Rewriting Workshops at UCLA Extension, Writer's Program, the largest writing program in America.

My hope in writing this book is that it will help you raise the level of your writing and improve your chances for selling your script.

Keep writing and keep thinking about writing.

Tom Lazarus, January 6, 2012
Los Angeles, California, U.S.A.

how to use this book

Your job as a screenwriter is to grab the reader by the throat early on and never let them go. There are more than a hundred topics in *The Last Word* that give you the tools to do that.

You should be able to use this book as a resource while preparing to write your script as well as when you write and rewrite it.

The idea for this book came from my teaching screenwriting and rewriting workshops. The wonderful thing about those workshops is that each writer learns not only from the notes on their script but from the notes on all the other scripts.

In many cases they take the lessons learned from notes on other scripts and apply them successfully to their script. That's the idea of *The Last Word*. I'm using my script notes to screenwriters as the jumping off point for the information in this book. The writing issues are real, not theoretical, with practical, real-world solutions.

If I had my way, you'd take each and every script note I've written to other writers and apply them to what you're doing and your writing, seeing if it's relevant and making the appropriate adjustments.

You'll notice that the most important information is covered a few times and in a few different ways. Sometimes I can be a little dense about learning new things, so the repetition is for emphasis, not a sign of my lapsing intellectual capabilities.

You also might notice that occasionally I'll drift into loony writing for just a moment. I trust you'll bear with me. It's my attempt to have this book be as much fun to read as it is for me to write.

Ultimately, *The Last Word* is about how to engage readers and keep them engaged in your script.

If you have a question that isn't covered in the book
and you're stuck, email me at:
LAZARUSTOM@AOL.COM
and I will promptly answer your question.

acknowledgements

I'd like to thank all my many students who have patiently put up with my take-no-prisoners approach to educating. More than once the jerk in me has bubbled to the surface and had to be beaten back with fiery torches. I appreciate the students' stamina and bravery in regard to this manner.

I thank Linda Venis, Ph.D., and Chae Ko at UCLA Extension Writer's Program, who have supported my unorthodox teaching style for these many years. I thank all the students who have unwittingly supplied grist for this book; their service, though unrewarded, is much appreciated.

I thank Stevie, my wife and partner, for listening patiently to my rants on scripts she doesn't care at all about and tempering my script notes so they are, at least, civil.

Thanks to Sol Weisel for pointing me in the right direction and to Michael Wiese and Ken Lee, who in a sea of rejection are a welcome port in the storm.

Finally, I thank my father, who set the bar as to who I should be as an educator and as a man.

'a' story

I was working with a writer on her first draft. Reading it was a struggle and a little frustrating. I emailed her:

> **I'm 35 pages in and still a little unclear what the story is. Is it about Rory and the invention? Rory going up the corporate ladder? Rory and Lynn? I think your script needs a sharper story focus.**
>
> **Compounding the problem is that the first six pages are about Angela, a minor character who doesn't return to the script. It's off-point and off-putting.**

I've read a ton of scripts and probably the most common problem I've encountered is that the 'A' story, the heart of the screenplay, is woefully undeveloped.

I wrote another writer:

> **I'm thirty pages in and no main story has shown itself. Right now, it's a series of scenes — not building on anything, not coalescing into a story — not resonating, just a collection of random scenes. You need to write more.** (*See* RESONANCE)
>
> **What do you want us to care about? Why are we here? In other words, what's the 'A' story?**

The biggest issue for me is I think you're trying to do too much — telling too much story and sacrificing the 'A' story because of it.

The screenwriter was spending valuable pages servicing the 'B' and 'C' and 'D' stories, and, unfortunately, had not developed the 'A' story fully. She had also laden the beginning of the script with the Unholy Three: backstory, set-up, and exposition — the three biggest reasons why reading scripts sometimes feel like slogging through Jell-O. By the time the writer gets around to servicing the 'A' story, we don't care anymore. The journey's not worth it to us. Big, big problem. Common problem.

I'm on page 41. It takes an awful long time getting here. I think you are telling too many stories and not telling the Frank/Sunny story enough.

I wrote another writer:
There seems to be a number of stories that may be fighting each other or at least could be presented cleaner. You have Betty's, Ellen's, then Reed's. Not sure Willie's story is needed. You're asking the reader/viewer to invest in this story and then it goes away. A mistake. *You should be focusing the beginning of your script exclusively on the 'A' story.*

The thing about the human brain is it wants to find story-order out of story-chaos. It's our nature and these scripts don't allow that — because nothing builds. Story elements should resonate, change, keep adding more and more information. You should be supplying new story and character material in every scene so our brains can work at piecing together the pieces into a larger overall story. It's the pleasure of reading or watching a story develop. It allows for interactivity, for involvement and engagement, and that's the ultimate goal. You have to provide the structure that allows that to happen.

And it's not just the openings that have to focus on the 'A' story.

**I'm up to the "Does Hiram remember Freda?" pages —
many seemingly endless pages devoted to something
that doesn't really progress or move the story forward.**

**We're basically halfway through the script and we're
still not focused enough on the 'A' story evolving. That's
what you're writing about, that's what you want us to
care about and we do. Now, your job is to satisfy our
need for that story.**

I wrote to another writer:
**We're forty pages in and you've talked about the 'A'
story only twice — just talked about it, mind you, not
really started telling it. There's too much flab in this
script. Too many scenes are set-ups or transitions. Not
tight enough storytelling. I think you have to get your
story going so much faster than you do.**

The "old school" way of writing screenplays had page after
page of set-up and exposition to open a script. Those days, my
friends, are over — way over. (*See* RISING ACTION)

**I'm 38 pages into the script and I'm not sure there's a
big reason to continue reading. Set-up and exposition
are boring and not a way to start the script. You have to
get your 'A' story up and running faster.**

These days, the contemporary structural motif is different
than the antiquated three-act structure: *You should be getting your story going first, then bring in your backstory and
exposition if you need to.* You have to grab us with the story
you're here to tell. Once you've hooked us into the main story
— what we're there to see — then you can introduce character
or environment or the dreaded backstory if you have to. In my
experience, very little or no backstory or exposition is needed.
(*See* BACKSTORY AND EXPOSITION)

■ EXERCISE 1 – THE LAST WORD ON ISOLATING THE 'A' STORY.

Any of this ring true to you? Been using the three-act structure and suddenly you're worried about your script? Good.

My suggestion is to take a step back from your screenplay, create a scene list from your existing pages focusing on just the 'A' story. Isolate the 'A' story and see if you can keep your scene list just that and get it so the action rises. (*See* BEGINNING YOUR SCREENPLAY)

The scene list allows you to deal with your script on a conceptual level. Once the new scene list is in shape, then go back to script pages and reconfigure them.

If you're starting a new script, make your first scene list just be 'A' story. That will keep the 'A' story in the center of your script where it needs to be. Once you have your 'A' story so that it satisfies, then start adding other story elements wherever needed.

action

I was fortunate to have as a guest in one of my Master Classes, an ex-head of production at one of the major studios. During his interview, I asked him if he read the action in screenplays.

He said, "Of course I do."

"Really?"

He smiled. "Well, most of the time I don't," he admitted, "I mostly read the dialogue. I get a sense of what the action is, but don't really read it."

The question is how do you get people to read it?

One of my screenwriters sent me this scene:

```
Sam throws a roundhouse left at Paulie. Paulie's
face smashes into the ground. Sam pounces on
him and starts pummeling his face again and
again. Fredric pulls Sam off Paulie. They fight
back and forth across the wharf knocking into
bales of hay and other boxes. Punch after punch
they throw at each other until Sam knees Paulie
in the groin crumbling him. Paulie climbs to
his feet only to be met by Sam's clenched fist
hitting him in the face.
```

Hard to read. Hard to follow. Hard to care.

Try it like this:

```
Sam throws a roundhouse left at Paulie.

Paulie's face smashes into the ground.

Sam pounces on him and starts pummeling his face
again and again.
```

> Fredric pulls Sam off Paulie.
>
> They fight back and forth across the wharf
> knocking into bales of hay and boxes.
>
> They throw punch after punch at each other until
> Sam knees Paulie in the groin crumbling him.
>
> Paulie climbs to his feet only to be met by
> Sam's clenched fist hitting him in the face.

Try thinking about writing action more visually. What's the shot? What does the camera see? And I describe the action and skip a space between the pieces of action. The different points of view. In effect, the different shots.

Another writer submitted the following:

> James reaches for the manuscript but instead
> grabs John's hands. James pushes John hard. The
> gun goes off and a bullet hits the wall behind
> James. James stumbles backward, falling into the
> large pool of rain water and drops his gun.

I wrote him:

Design this differently, please. Separate the lines as if they were camera shots, but DO NOT call the shots. Write this fully. It's a big moment. Make more of it.

Here's the rewrite:

> James reaches for the manuscript, but he grabs
> John's hands.
>
> They struggle.
>
> James smashes John and the gun goes off with a
> BANG.
>
> A bullet explodes into the wall behind James.
>
> James staggers backward as the gun SKITTERS
> across the floor.

```
Stunned, John falls backwards into the large
pool of rain water.
```

Detailing the action precisely and clearly lets the reader better participate in the screenplay.

Another writer wrote:

```
They're getting the bullion, running out of the
building, running to the car, into the car,
pulling away…
```

None of this was written anywhere nearly enough. You're giving us "chapter headings" instead of detailing the scenes. These are the money scenes — the big action scenes — the gold of your screenplay — and you have to write them so we can see, feel, experience and enjoy them. Be more specific. And while you're rewriting — get your format correct!

His rewrite was a good one:

```
EXT. SECOND NATIONAL BANK — DAY
The door of the bank kicks open and the gang
runs out of the building with the bullion.

EXT. PARKING LOT — DAY
The gang dashes to the van.

INT. VAN — DAY
The gang leaps in, slam shut the doors.

EXT. PARKING LOT — DAY
The van SCREECHES into the street barely missing
oncoming traffic and speeds away up the block.
```

Another issue is *not* writing action.
For example:

```
The chase persists down the avenue.
```

Can action be written any less dramatically?
What do I see? What do I film? Be specific. More detailed writing in this section, please.

The same writer again:

> He undresses her with his eyes.

Again, what do we see? You're describing what he's doing but not what we're seeing on the screen. Is he looking up and down her body and smiling? Is he focusing on parts of her body and smiling? Is he looking at her and sneering? Give us a little more, please.

■ EXERCISE 2 – THE LAST WORD ON REWRITING ACTION.

Take the following blocks of action and space them properly so the page isn't dense and it's easy to follow as well as easy to read.

> EXT. VENICE SPEEDBOAT RIDES — DAY
> Andy Pasta backs his car down next to the boardwalk and slowly begins parking. Al and Johnny arrive at the Duesenberg. They both reach for the passenger side door.
>
> Al LAUGHS and climbs in. Johnny jumps behind the wheel, starts up the Dusie and with the SCREECHING OF TIRES heads inland. Capone's loving it.
>
> INT. BLACK FOUR-DOOR — DAY
> Chief Davis rides shotgun. There are two COPS in back. They're stalled behind Pasta's slowly parking car.
>
> EXT. VENICE SPEEDBOAT RIDES — DAY
> Grinning from ear to ear, Andy Pasta finally parks, then waves at the black four-doors. After Chief Davis flips him off, they speed away after the Duesenberg.
>
> EXT. WEST LA — DAY
> Orange groves. The occasional clapboard farm house and the Duesenberg roaring North toward a four-door Reo. Johnny is surprised that it's Rubio and Fittipaldi in the Reo as they fly past. Rubio's head whips around as the Duesenberg roars by. He jams on the brakes and power slides into a U-turn. Chief Davis's two tailing Police four-doors swerve off the road to

avoid a collision with Rubio. Johnny floors it.
Al's cigar flies out of the car and he cracks
up. As the three cars close in, the Duesenberg
roars away.

■ EXERCISE 3 — THE LAST WORD ON REWRITING YOUR EXISTING ACTION.

Take one of your action blocks, the densest one in your screen-play, and re-space it, making it read easier and look lighter on the page. Then, re-think it, spend some time trying to go beyond the first draft of writing, and think about the most visually detailed way to present the action. Visualize the action in the shot and describe it without actually calling the shot. This is what you should be doing with all the action sequences in your screenplay.

acts of god

A writer in one of my classes was writing a story in which his main character traveled back in time where most of the story takes place. I was reading and everything was going fine, the story started right off the top and I was happy — until I read:

```
EXT. MOUNTAINS — DAY
Lionel is walking up the mountain trail, past
the logs, and waterfalls, when suddenly there's
a bolt of lightning. Lionel is surrounded by a
violet aura, then he disappears.

EXT. LAND OF NORR — DAY
Lionel appears in a violet cloud next to a
fountain in a city square.
```

I wrote to the writer:

Not sure about your device to get Lionel back in time. My problem is it's purely an Act of God. Lionel does nothing to get himself back. It's not dependent on any story beat that came before it which makes me very concerned. In the best of all possible worlds, the device sending Lionel back would be integral to the story, coming from within the story rather than unmotivated from the outside.

Of course, Acts of God don't literally have to be a bolt of lightning from the heavens. Acts of God — be they a random car crash, a piece of space junk falling on our antagonist at just the appropriate moment and saving our hero, your main character hitting his head and suddenly having second sight allowing him to see the hidden treasure map on the parchment — are all pretty much life happening to your main character from outside the story. Nothing the main character is doing causes the big change in the story to happen. Better storytelling is when the change is caused by the main character or comes from within the story with something you've already set up.

adapting novels

I was working with a writing team who were adapting a novel they'd optioned and sent me their first draft for notes.

> **Hey Guys —**
> **The big issue for me in your draft is that you've tried to capture the feeling of the novel and have depended on voice over — the voice in the mind of the main character of the novel — to carry the burden of storytelling. I do not believe this is the best solution to adapting this novel. It breaks one of the few unbreakable rules of screenwriting: _Show don't tell._ (_See_ SHOWING RATHER THAN TELLING) Now, get back up on your chairs and let's figure out what to do.**
>
> **Your job — which you haven't done adequately, yet — is to find images, scenes and behavior for the words and actions in the book — not depend on voice over. (_Please see_ VOICE OVER)**
>
> **The best scenes from the novel have Lloyd telling us about the story action rather than letting us experience the story by seeing the story action take place. That's what movies are for. This is a very big note as it addresses the basic point of view and film language of your script.**
>
> **My suggestion is to experiment with one of the most important scenes in the book — the assassination. Instead of having Lawrence tell Mary about it, let's see**

Lawrence's participation in the scene as it goes down. The telling of it works in the book, but not so much in the script. You have to re-think how you're approaching this adaptation.

Another issue you should start thinking about is that novels spend a great deal of time in the heads of their characters, what they're thinking and feeling, and put voice to all that. Movies don't do that, other than occasionally in voice over. We're not inside the heads of our characters *so they have to express themselves by their behavior.* You have to start thinking that way if you want to tell this story cinematically rather than novelistically.

Later on in the script, the writer wrote:

```
He has the gift of an astonishingly clever brain
and the watchful eye and tracking ability of a
natural born hunter.
```

One of the other issues in your script is that you describe internal processes that are unable to be filmed. *Your job is to report what we see and hear on the screen.* (*See* INTERNAL PROCESSES)

LOYALTY TO SOURCE MATERIAL WHEN ADAPTING

I have had many writers who are adapting literary material to a screenplay or are telling a true story, or writing an autobiographical script. One such writer was writing a script about her grandmother returning to the small town where she grew up.

My problem with the script was that the story didn't arc, the structure didn't work. It was just scene after scene with no overall vision or structural motif.

I wrote to her and told her she'd need to impose some structure and plotting of action to start a build in the story.

She wrote back:

"The facts don't lend themselves to any structure but the one I'm using. So I'm going to stick with what I have."

Needless to say, I wrote her back.

I understand the problem. At some point, writers writing from source material of any kind — including a true story — have to make a decision: be true to reality and write a script that doesn't work, or *shift your loyalty to the script*, allowing yourself license to change the facts or reality so that the script works. Your loyalty has to be your script. It's a hard transition to make. Sometimes, it's called "poetic license."

Writers who tell me they have to stay close to "the truth" always have me questioning what the truth is.

Your grandmother's memories? Truth?

Aren't memories shaded by time?

Television interviews? Truth?

Doesn't television show only part of the truth? You're not looking at raw footage when you see interviews. Selections have been made. Someone has edited it. It's the editor's truth. The "truth" is subjective.

At some point, most writers writing their true story, or adapting a book, or writing about an actual event, or a real person, have to give up their loyalty to the truth in deference to their script. Why wouldn't you be willing to do that?

FOLLOW-UP: The writer made some adjustments, but was concerned that her family was going to read it and be mad at her and she was feeling guilty about the changes she had already made. She stuck to the truth and her script remained unsatisfying.

a kick in the ass

In one of my Advanced Rewriting Workshops I was working with a writer who was extremely confident about his script. He felt parts of it were "perfect." (Perfect? Really? After only two drafts? It takes me twenty drafts to get to "perfect.") And the rest of his script, according to him, needed only some modest "tweaks."

My first set of notes for him was met with major resistance, something I've run across since I began teaching the Advanced Rewriting Workshops and recognize as Writer's Resistance — the totally understandable yet sometimes desperate clinging to the original draft because of time and passion invested. The writer disagreed with many of my notes. He presented a carefully thought out rationale for everything he wrote.

This was going to take some time.

I started by explaining that an airtight rationale of why you wrote something doesn't necessarily make it good script.

He reluctantly did a few tweaks/suggestions I had made about speeding up his script — less set-up and more directly into the 'A' story, orienting the opening a little bit better toward the main character so we know who the movie is about, and adding more 'A' story action. His new draft was better, but it was pretty much the same old same old, definitely not "perfect."

It was time for me to strike. Sometimes I think of myself as a screenwriting Superhero swooping in to save the day. Well, actually I don't, but I like the image.

THE LAST WORD ■ LAZARUS

The big note I'm feeling about your script is that you're being way too timid in your approach to the rewrite. *Your job as a screenwriter is to reach the potential of your idea*. Your good idea has to be fully realized and, simply put, you're not there yet. And, until you are, you're not finished.

One of Hollywood's major script doctors told me he's hired because other writers with good ideas and scripts that get bought by the studios "Don't have the chops or wherewithal to deliver a finished, fully realized script." I didn't want this writer's script to fall into that category.

I think you have to crack this script open (I know you think parts are perfect and the sense I get about the rest is that you think it's a lot better than it is). Your script has to be a slam dunk to get bought and made and it's not there yet.

You've got to dig deeper and *maximize every scene*. Fully develop your characters, make sure every word of your dialogue rings true. You're not doing that — and until you do, you're being way too easy on yourself.

He wrote me back: *"Duly noted."*
I know the brush-off when I read it.
I wrote him back.
What do you have to lose by responding to these notes in a new draft? How long would it take you? A week? Two weeks? What if I'm right? What if it makes your script ten percent or twenty percent better? Isn't it worth it?

And if you don't like it as much? You can always throw out the draft, curse me up and down as that jerk screenwriting instructor who doesn't know his ass from his asterisk, and go on your merry way to Hollywood stardom.

FOLLOW-UP: Kicking and screaming, the screenwriter did a number of major rewrites, improved the script a lot and ended up pleased with his final draft.

The writer wrote me:

"At the beginning, I fought and struggled with each critique, each suggestion. But, eventually it made my writing and my script stronger. In such a short time, my script has improved. Thanks."

My work here is done. Up, up and away....

antagonists

A writer in one of my on-site classes was writing a script about aliens working for the FBI. I was interested in the script because I'd never read anything quite like it. When I read the draft it was, disappointingly, woefully lacking.

Simply put, your antagonist isn't bad enough. His nefarious plot? To destroy the bond market. It's small potatoes — hardly what we make movies about. (*Please see* WHAT SHOULD YOU BE WRITING ABOUT?)

Sure we hate the Wall Street types that are ruining America and they clearly are the bad guys, but I'm not sure destroying the bond market is what we make movies about. It might be different if this were a *Wall Street*-type movie, but it's not. It's an alien run and jump action script. (*See* WHAT WE WRITE MOVIES ABOUT)

Dig deeper and spend some time coming up with a list of other bad things that the antagonist could be involved in. What about a plan that will bring down the total economy of the United States? The world? What about a scheme that threatens the lives of millions? Chemicals? Pollution of the water supply? Smallpox? Don't censor your ideas. How does the antagonist threaten our hero?

He doesn't.
Does the antagonist jeopardize the hero in any way?
He doesn't.
Let it flow and see what happens.

Conventional screenwriting wisdom has it that the badder the bad guy, the better the good guy. It's true. The more the hero has to overcome, the better hero he is.

OTHER NOTES ON THE ANTAGONIST

The Antagonist is the Yin to the Protagonist's Yang.

The Antagonist should have an arc — some place for his badness to get badder.

You don't want your Bad Guy to be a hundred percent bad at the beginning of the script because his behavior will be one-noted throughout the rest of the script. The character will have nowhere to develop to, nowhere to evolve.

Your characters should have more colors than just the role they play. My bias is that the Bad Guy should be a not-so-bad guy at the beginning of your script so that his arc has a bigger move — from good to bad. With that being said, I've seen it work fabulously well to have the bad guy be introduced as heinous and remain heinous throughout. It's your call.

appropriate language

Does a 12-year-old boy turn to his pal and says he's feeling "melancholy"?

In 1904, do college frat brothers really say "hang out"?

Would the gas station attendant in Boise, Idaho, really use the word "Herculean"?

I don't think so.

Make sure your characters are speaking appropriately for their age, the year they're living, their education, upbringing and their position in life. All of those influences shade the way a character talks and his vocabulary.

There are, of course, exceptions, but the bottom line is: the language has to ring true. Be authentic. That's the ultimate test.

army takes the town

One of my students wrote:

```
EXT. JHEZZO VALLEY — DAY
Brooke and the other hikers move down the
winding trail, arrive in camp, they put up
tents, lay out the picnic table, have a swim and
settle down to a dinner of hot dogs and beans
when the pack of red-eyed wolves descend on
them from the phalanx of flying saucers and the
battle ensues.
```

59 words.
No big deal, right?
Wrong.
It's a very big deal.

Let's analyze this the way Production — the people responsible for physical shooting, scheduling and budgeting a movie — does, and see what it entails.

First, the format is awful and will make the people in production pull their hair out. Each time the crew moves the camera to a new set-up, it's a new scene, with a new scene number and its own place on the schedule. It's how we keep track of the thousands of individual pieces of film or video.

What are the different locations in the scene?

```
EXT. JEZZO VALLEY TRAIL — DAY
EXT. CAMPSITE — DAY
EXT. PICNIC AREA — DAY
EXT. THE LAKE — DAY
EXT. CAMPSITE - NIGHT
```

So much more complicated: not one scene but five. Both Day and Night. Mountains. Lake. Campsite. Lots of traveling. Maybe three days of production.

Then, Production has to scout and select the locations, cast the extras, find the props, train the stunt people, provide the transportation, rent equipment, accommodations for cast and crew, plan for the catering including getting some prop hot dogs and beans, apply for permits for all of the above, casting some real wolves or creating CGI wolves and design and execute the special effects for a "phalanx of flying saucers."

The price tag?

Two million dollars.

Fifty-nine words equals two million dollars.

How much do you think "The Army takes the town" would cost?

Why is this important? It may not matter so much on your rough draft, but down the line, when professionals read and evaluate your script, such blatant generalizations that so affect the budget are warning signs of an amateur, which is the last thing you want anyone to think as they read your script.

I [B]

backstory

Let's cut to the chase: I hate backstory.

Why, you ask?

Because eighty-five percent of it is unnecessary. Most of the time we don't need the backstory at all and it absolutely destroys the forward momentum of your script.

Believe it or not, we actually can get to know and love characters without knowing their backstory, just like real people. We judge them by their behavior, what we experience of them.

When I fell in love with my wife — that's a whole other book — I didn't know her family, medical, or relationship history. I didn't know about her awful mother, her horrible sister, or her wonderful father. I didn't know where she went to school, if she brushed after every meal, which side of the bed she slept on or about that mole — or what I hope is a mole — on the back of her leg. All I knew was what I experienced with her: she was beautiful, she made me laugh, turned me on, and was smart. I was hooked without the dreaded backstory.

Reader/viewers across the globe today are so sophisticated and hip that when they see a character on screen and see their clothes, their car, the kind of place they live, they get it and they get it fast.

To explain how they were brought up and where they went to school and when they fell down and skinned their knee is added baggage.

The Social Network — Aaron Sorkin's fabulous script, David Fincher directing — presents the Mark Zuckerberg character first in a bar filled with young people and then we see him in a hoodie, Gap t-shirt, jeans and flip-flops running across the Harvard campus in the snow. We know exactly who that main character is in surprising depth. He's young, a student, preoccupied, so the weather is unimportant. Fashion and appearance are irrelevant to this character. He's energy-driven because he runs. He's smart 'cause he's at Harvard. And after that first scene where he was brilliant, strange and difficult — we know this guy.

We don't know his parents, if he wore braces, if he has a bratty sister, an abusive father, where he went to school, who he dated, or if his sled was named Rosebud. But, nonetheless, we totally get him. Take a look at the movie and see. By the way, it's a terrific movie. (*See* MOVIE RECOMMENDATIONS)

I was working on a rewrite with a screenwriter in my Master Class on Screenwriting whose opening didn't work.

She was writing about a girl who has a painful, obsessive crush on her teacher. The writer opened the script with a long sequence of the main character as a child enduring a series of events she carries with her later in life. In other words, the cause of her obsession. I suggested her fifteen-page backstory introduction wasn't needed as it was, in fact, backstory, which is rarely needed, and didn't involve the Big Cheese actress, the main character, who we'll be paying millions of dollars. Plus, the backstory wasn't news because it's pretty much universally accepted that what happens in our childhood affects us later in life and, more importantly, the unnecessary backstory effectively pushed off the start of the story some fifteen pages which was truly a bad idea. I suggested she try an alternate, non-backstory opening.

She wrote:

"Hi, Tom. I thought about it and I would like to work on the script without rearranging the basic structure."

You think I wrote her back?

You tell me readers don't think the script works though the pitch does — yet you're unwilling to change it? I don't get it.

"I'm comfortable with the way it is."

Well, I wasn't ready to let it go.
What exactly do you have to lose trying something different? You can always put it back the way it was. Writing is a plastic medium, not like sculpting in marble where you make a cut and you can never go back. Screenwriting allows you the luxury of experimenting, of trying things. Take advantage of it.

Try your script without the backstory and if you don't like it, don't use it. It'll take you how long? A day. You can't spare a day to potentially open your script more effectively?

Wait for it....
"Okay, I'll try it."

FOLLOW-UP: The writer came back in two days with a new opening — no backstory — and her script worked really well.

What do I want you to take away from that example?
Try different approaches. Take chances. It costs you nothing. If one out of five times it results in a positive addition to the script, it's worth it. What do you have to lose?

To another writer:
I'm reading along in your well-written script and liking it when suddenly on pages 34 and 35 the script screeches to a halt. Why? Inexplicably you start telling Abe's backstory, his upbringing, his childhood traumas. All unnecessary. Too dense. I was enjoying the script just fine without knowing any of the backstory. Do you really need it? Please think about it. It's lots and lots of talk and scenes without the main character who's suddenly being played by some snot-nosed kid actor.

Another way to look at backstory:

A twelve-page backstory/flashback?!?! If you took this out of the movie — would it change the basic story?

I argue that usually it won't. And if it won't — you have to ask yourself the question: what the hell's it doing in there?

I write to another writer:

Try something for me. Save the draft you have, then take the first twenty pages and do a quick rewrite eliminating backstories and all the exposition and let the story tell itself. Let me know what you think.

The writer ended up taking out most of the backstory but couldn't let go of all of it. That writer is now selling women's undergarments at Fancy Fashions in Toledo, Ohio.

Well, not really, but I'm sure the script would have read better with all of the backstories out of there.

I don't get to use the word "undergarments" enough in my life.

beginning
your screenplay

I was working with a new writer and he had no idea how to start writing a screenplay. He was feeling a bit overwhelmed. Totally understandable.

This is what I told him:

Okay, you have an idea for a script. You're excited. You can see it. It's a movie! Where do you start? Let me tell you what I do — and it works.

From the moment the idea occurs to me I start writing things down. I open four documents in my computer: IDEAS, SCENES, CHARACTER, and MISCELLANEOUS. Now, I'm ready.

My idea — well, it's something about a boxer and a referee. I list those two characters in my CHARACTERS file. It's about the boxer getting injured in a fight refereed by our other character.

Names? I put the Boxer's name as JOHNNY BRAVO and the referee's name as SINCLAIR.

My mind is racing...ideas...characters...scenes — so I start adding to the lists. I never censor my ideas. I let them flow. I never say "That's a lousy idea." It may indeed be lousy, but if I don't censor it, and write it down on one of my lists, it may open the door to a great idea, or, because I've downloaded the idea onto my lists, it has left room for a truly good idea to enter my mind.

THE LAST WORD ■ LAZARUS

So I let myself go:

Snippets of dialogue "I remember you — no, I don't."

The image of a mouthpiece being spit out.

A groupie seduces boxers.

The boxer shows signs of brain damage.

I put that in my SCENES file with an asterisk. An important scene. And I flow with ideas — for a day — for two days — for a week, then, inevitably, because my mind instinctively starts to search for order out of the chaos, the movie starts to coalesce and I start organizing a scene list, a chronology of scenes. No details — just the conceptual load of the scene.

What does the scene do?

Why is it in the script?

What's the information?

How does it move the story forward?

I know I have the BRAVO GETS INJURED IN RING. SINCLAIR REFS.

That's a scene.

Which one is my main character? I think: Bravo gets brain damage.

The referee has a moral issue — does he let the brain damaged fighter fight?

Interesting character dilemma. I think of *Rain Man*. Who's the main character? Not Dustin Hoffman, but Tom Cruise. I decide Sinclair, the referee, is the protagonist. I think, at least for now, I've made the correct decision.

Another sure scene: FIVE YEARS LATER, SINCLAIR TO REF A SECOND BOUT WITH BRAVO — SEES BRAIN DAMAGE. A key scene. Has to come near the end. Maybe the end of Act 2. (Note: though I'm using RISING ACTION as my structural motif, I use the Acts to indicate where a scene lives within the landscape of the script.) Maybe in the middle of Act 3. I put it both places in my scene chronology with a question mark.

We know what we know. And when we know more, things change. Creating your scene list is a process of learning about your movie, about your characters and constantly applying it to evolving pages.

Okay, now I'm getting excited. I've got a pretty good idea of what the overall movie is — at least so far — so I create a LOG LINE. The log line is a very valuable screenwriter's tool. *The log line is the essence of the movie idea: one or two sentences that say precisely what the movie is.*

Some examples of log lines:

Titanic — A love story on the doomed super liner.

Lawrence of Arabia — T.E. Lawrence goes to India and becomes a legend.

2001: A Space Odyssey — A mission to Jupiter goes wrong and the crew is forced to fight for their lives and immortality.

Citizen Kane — A reporter tries to find out why publishing giant Charles Foster Kane said "Rosebud" right before he died and learns about his life.

The log line for my idea:

SINCLAIR REFS A FIGHT WHERE JOHNNY BRAVO GETS HURT. FIVE YEARS LATER, THE REF IS TO OFFICIATE ANOTHER MATCH WITH BRAVO BUT NOTICES HE'S BRAIN DAMAGED AND THEIR LIVES BECOME INTERTWINED.

Notice the log line leads with my main character. The rule: *Tell your story through the main character.* (*Please see* MAIN CHARACTERS)

My log line is not as concise as the others, but, as I've said, it's a process so I don't worry about it and keep moving forward. I will shape and hone the log line — and detail out "Their lives become intertwined" — and then, as I write, judge everything against it.

I know that the log line is my 'A' story. My spine. The story I want to tell. I know I seriously have to question the validity of a scene if it doesn't, in some way, involve or relate to the log line.

Where do I want to start the movie? I'm not sure, so I put a place holder MOVIE STARTS HERE in my scene list.

Here's the start of the list:
MOVIE STARTS HERE
INTRODUCE SINCLAIR REFEREEING
A PERSONAL SINCLAIR SCENE
ANOTHER SCENE TO BE DETERMINED
THE BRAVO — BRAIN INJURY FIGHT SCENE

Okay, I'm off and running. And I don't care if it's wrong. And I don't care if I have to change everything. *The idea is don't censor and keep moving forward.* I sprinkle information into my scene list and it's getting longer and longer, more detailed. By the way, there is no correct number of scenes.

The story development will continue through scene list, script, shooting and editing — always refining the story, rounding it out, maturing it.

To get a better perspective on the information I've amassed, *I code the scene list.*

I put a circle next to all the boxing scenes.

I put an 'S' next to all the scenes with Sinclair.

A 'B' next to all the scenes with Bravo.

I have a love interest for Sinclair: Genie — so I put an X next to her scenes. And so on.

After a while, I take my scene list — which now stretches to three double-spaced pages — scenes coded — and read the movie like a music score. I can see the rhythms, the ebb and flow of the story as they roll by on my screen.

I print the pages out, color code some more information — talk scenes, doctor scenes, love scenes — and tape them together so I can see the whole thing at once — to really see the letter and color rhythms of the screenplay as a single entity. I find this incredibly helpful. It's another way I keep trying to understand and get perspective on what I'm doing.

Now that I've lived with the story, re-written the scene list a bunch of times, I'm chomping at the bit — I can't hold back — I've got to write — so I write FADE IN: and start pouring out script pages using my scene list as the jumping off point.

I allow things to change in the writing of the script. It's another facet of the process of writing this screenplay. I know as long as I stay near the spine of the story, as indicated by the scene list, I can't go very wrong.

Using all that pent-up creative energy, I power forward writing script pages. I crank them out. I don't stop to rewrite. I use the enthusiasm I have to build a page count, to establish a flow — and I don't look back.

The truth of why I don't look back? In my mind's eye, the script pages I've written are great.

The reality of the pages?

They're rough draft, crude pages at best. So I have nothing to gain by dampening the fantasy of 'great' pages with the reality.

If I don't know something or haven't got it solved, I don't let it stop me — I write a temporary solution — a place holder — to the problem and power on.

Finally, I stop. I've written five pages or fifteen or thirty pages. Whatever. I take a breath and read the pages and start rewriting them.

After they're rewritten a couple of times to make them readable and more coherent, closer to what was in my mind's eye, then move forward again to the next batch of pages, take a breath, rewrite them a couple of times, then move forward in this manner until I write FADE OUT.

The key for me is organization — epitomized by the scene list. This scene list, working as a spine or anchor, allows me to be totally creative and free while I'm writing because I know I'm always close to the core of the script.

being a screenwriter

A frustrated, overwhelmed student wrote me:

"My story is extremely hard to work on because the original story was mostly adventures forced by external events. Here I'm intending to reconcile external forces and internal forces to get a result."

I wrote her back:

If it were easy it wouldn't be any fun. Take a deep breath. Stay away from your computer for a day. Think about your story. Don't think about it. Whichever is right for you. In any event, let it percolate in your brain then come back to it a little fresher, a little more positive and see what happens.

Screenwriting is tremendous fun partially, I think, because it is so hard. And when you do it well and succeed it's very satisfying. I feel extremely fortunate to have been able to make a really good living as a screenwriter. To spend my work life creating stories and characters and solving creative problems is a wonderful way to make this journey.

As good as the good is — there's a lot bad, too. Out of work, unloved, calls not returned, feeling that Hollywood is passing you by, a life of crushing rejections, disappointments and snubs, long periods with no money at all, and, of course, the exhausting pursuit of perfectionism. (*See* PERFECTIONISM)

Here are some of the things I've learned — pearls of wisdom, to be presumptuous — that have made my life as a screenwriter a little easier:

As I've mentioned before and will mention any number of times more — screenwriting is a process. **Be bold. Try different things.** If they don't work, who cares? You can always rewrite it.

The most important thing to do is to identify and sell the 'A' story. If that's satisfying and full and rich, you win. If you can put in other things without diluting the 'A' story — do it. Try it and see how it works.

When I begin writing a screenplay, **I experiment** with different takes on the same scene, push my characters into different places to see how it feels, to see how they react, to see what happens. There is no good or bad, right or wrong at this point. **I follow my instincts.** I don't censor myself at all.

You know why?

Because I'm coming back to revisit this writing again — many times. Many, many times.

I'll try dialogue and action on for size. If, when I rewrite, it doesn't feel right, it's gone. **If it feels good, it stays.** Notice that I use the word "feel." I urge screenwriters to work out of the right side of their brain and get in touch with their feelings about the writing.

Some writers I've worked with approach screenwriting as if they're looking for the secret formula they feel exists that would allow them to write the great script. No matter what the screenwriting gurus tell you, there's no magic formula for screenwriting success. You can't worry about it. All you can do is write. And keep writing. And keep writing.

I once had a student who came to class and said he had combined the elements of the top ten movies of all time and wanted to write a script using those box office proven elements.

I told him to write it in another class. (*See* WHAT SHOULD YOU BE WRITING ABOUT?)

I had another screenwriter who wanted me to tell him what to do — exactly what to do. Screenwriting doesn't work that way. There are so many variables, so many things that go wrong in the telling of the story. Every story is different, with different characters and diverse behaviors and actions. To try and formulate a winning strategy for writing your script is a pretty hapless venture. **Each story has its own integrity.** Your job is to find it and write to it.

You've seen enough movies, television shows, short films, read enough books and stories to know what you like and don't like. The challenge is to **find the place in your gut that knows good from bad**, right from wrong, what is truthful what is not — listen to it and write to it.

I have a student in one of my classes now who told another student about her script: "They're not going to buy that."

I asked him if he really knew what "they" were going to buy? And if he did, how come he didn't do that and sell scripts? He's never sold a screenplay.

I've been writing for what seems like a hundred years sometimes and, as I previously mentioned, it still takes me twenty drafts — that's right — **twenty drafts** to reach a first draft. I write ten drafts to reach a rough draft. In these early drafts, I try different things, write whole passages that don't work, that I delete. I'm not deleting mistakes. I'm deleting experiments. All good.

So after about ten drafts, I send my rough draft out to a couple of my readers, who tell me it's lousy and that I have to work harder, dig deeper, crank it up. That's their job. They're smart and sensitive enough to say nice things as well. The custom in Hollywood, and I'm sure elsewhere, is to open a notes session with compliments — at least for a while — before you get to the tough stuff. I do whatever notes of theirs I think will improve my script and continue rewriting.

The mantra that runs through my mind, driving me on — a truism about screenwriting: **The more you work on your screenplay the better it gets.**

After ten more drafts, where I've struggled to round out the script, mature it, to reach the potential in every scene, to make format, grammar, everything perfect. Then, I send it out and move on to the next project.

For me, writing first thing in the morning — before my mind clouds with life — is the most productive. Before I open email, or check my phone messages, before I exercise or play with the dogs, I make myself a soy latte and write. First thing in the morning is by far the most productive time of the day.

Over the years, I've learned how to survive emotionally and psychologically in Hollywood so I didn't end up floating face down in Norma Desmond's swimming pool. (See *Sunset Boulevard*, and I mean the movie. It's fantastic)

I don't get my ego strokes only if someone likes the script, or it gets bought, or it gets made. That's a losing game. Those things are totally out of my control and, frankly, for all of us, it's such a long shot, I'd hate to only feel good if someone else approves of what I do. So **I take my ego satisfaction from what I can control — the screenplay itself**. If I have reached the potential of the idea, given the script my all, done the best I can — then I'm happy.

Rewriting is where screenwriters live. It's in the rewrite where, like that sculptor with his piece of raw marble, the screenwriter works with his material, taking away what doesn't work to reveal the final screenplay.

My favorite Pablo Picasso quote:
"Art is the elimination of the unnecessary."
It's perfect for screenwriters.

A lot of writers ask: *"How do I know when my screenplay is finished?"*

It's a real issue for a lot of writers. It's easy to think that once you've finished your draft, Spell Checked it and had your mother read it and love it, that you're finished. Well, it ain't that easy.

One of the major issues in many, many of the screenplays I read is, simply, they've been sent out too soon. They're not finished. Sometimes it feels the writer has gotten to the end, typed FADE OUT, and sent the script out. Screenwriting is hard. It takes time to mature your writing.

I consider a script I'm writing finished when:
- It has fulfilled the promise of the original idea.
- Every facet of the script has reached its potential.
- When I read it and I feel satisfied.
- When I read it from the start and make only piddling changes.
- When I read it and the page count doesn't change.
- When I can't think of how to change it anymore.

You usually have only one chance with a reader, or producer, or contest, or wherever you're sending your script. You only shoot yourself in the foot if you send out a script that isn't ready.

I'm fortunate to have a reader who not only offers honest feedback, but is a second pair of eyes to check for spelling, missing words, and inconsistencies. Invaluable.

The rule is: **Never send out a script until it's finished and perfect.**

be specific

A screenwriter sent me pages. This is the first scene in his screenplay:

```
INT. MASTER BEDROOM — NIGHT
Immaculate. Wealthy. A bed with one occupant.
HEDY PIERCE is beautiful as the painting she
stands in front of.
TITLES begin.
```

I had problems before the titles.

I wrote the screenwriter:

The problem with using generic, non-specific, maddeningly vague words is that I can't see what the scene looks like. "Immaculate?" Does that mean sterile, or cluttered but perfectly clean? "Wealthy?" Does that mean Louis the XIVth ornate gold French antiques or sleek Corbusier chrome and leather pieces? And the "painting?" A Rembrandt or Elvis on velvet? You need to stop writing words and write what you see.

The job of a screenwriter is to report what's on the screen, what we see specifically, not generically.

Army ants versus insects.

Leopards versus animals.

Spruce trees versus trees.

Leaves and twigs versus forest debris.

Sharpened stone lashed to a branch versus spear.

Copperware and baskets selling in the square versus selling various items.

A peach versus a piece of fruit.

■ EXERCISE 4 — THE LAST WORD ON BEING SPECIFIC.

Take a crack at rewriting the following making the writing much more specific.

```
EXT. CITY — DAY
Cars in the street.

INT. STORE — DAY
MORRIS, a tall man, enters. He has a package and
sets it on the counter. LEANORA, the proprietor,
enters from the back.

                    LEANORA
        I told you to not come in here.

                    MORRIS
        I hate you.

Leanora takes out a weapon.

                    LEANORA
        Do you think I care?

Morris attacks Leanora. They fight. Morris wins,
empties the cash register and leaves.

Leanora climbs to her feet and freaks out.
```

■ EXERCISE 4A — THE LAST WORD ON SEEING YOUR SCRIPT.

If your writing is generic versus specific and you can't "see" what you're writing about: take ten pages of your script and rewrite it with as many specific rather than generic descriptions that you can write. My guess is you'll "see" a much different script than you had before. (*See* THE DEAL)

bookends

Too many scripts I read these days open with bookends — framing scenes — usually part of the climax — as a hook at the very beginning of the script.

Frankly, I don't get it. Why do screenwriters take the juicy climax to their script and run it out of context at the beginning of the script before we know what's going on or are invested in the characters?

It's a mystery.

I have two theories: one is that screenwriters who do this are insecure about the story they're telling and don't have faith in the first pages of their screenplay so they feel they have to give away the climax at the beginning to hook the reader.

My response?

Write a better opening!

The second theory is that they've seen bookends in other scripts they've read and in movies they've seen so it must be the right thing to do. Well, it isn't.

I wrote to a writer I was working with:

I don't think the bookend/flash forward opening works at all. In these most important three pages of the script, you ask us to invest in Peter, a warm and fuzzy old man, who next appears 110 pages later, and we get a history of the reporter (?!) — someone we'll never see again — and introduce a location at length that isn't important at all. And what do you get? In my mind, you get a delay

in opening your script and misdirection for your reader/ viewer.

The reason I don't think bookends like this are the optimum way to open a script is because the reader/viewer doesn't know not to invest in these pages. Like all readers, they commit to these characters and these first pages, then the rug is pulled out from under them and they don't return to this universe for 110 pages. Doesn't work for me. Doesn't make the reader trust the screenwriter.

Another writer I was working with opened his script with a three-page graveyard scene where a man is axe murdered after finding some kind of a relic. It's all very mysterious and inexplicable.

I know you really like the graveyard scene — who doesn't like an axe murder? — but you should cut it. You open with a scene that doesn't introduce your main characters or the 'A' story. Cut it.

The writer explained:
"The scene pays off on page 124 successfully bookending the script."

A scene that pays off a hundred and twenty pages later doesn't "successfully" anything — because it starts your script off on the wrong foot. It confuses rather than informs. It doesn't involve continuing characters — or more importantly the main character — and we don't learn anything. It's an intellectual conceit.

Page one is too important to waste on non-relevant material. You have to weigh what you get and what you lose by putting a scene like this at the very beginning of your story. Your script has to get to the 'A' story or your readers are going to tune out — like I did. You're dealing with professional readers in the world of screenwriting. Get to it.

But, God bless him, he wouldn't give up. He said what he was trying to do in those early, excruciatingly slow pages was *"To illustrate Prince Valiant's everyday world."*

I know. It's set-up. Where's the 'A' story? That's what the reader's looking for. After the questionable opening, there are ten pages of characters who don't continue on in the movie, colorful characters who aren't part of the 'A' story.

The screenwriter explains that these characters *"Present the theme."*

I angrily reach for my gun, but think better of it and email him back:

Please, don't have anyone "present" your theme. Let it seep out of your pages as subtext. These ten pages of unimportant characters and irrelevant action should be cut. We're here to see your log line. Your main character goes back in time to protect Prince Valiant, who is in danger. Good log line. Until you get to that story — we don't care so much.

The way to think about it is: **Start your story and get it up and running, then, if you need to set up anything, do it as you tell the story**.

FOLLOW-UP: The writer was willing to try a new opening and he ended up pleased with it.

 C

calling shots

Way too many writers I read call shots.

    CLOSE UP on Magda's curling fingernail.

Or:

    PAN TO REVEAL
    A photograph of Lucianne as a horrible little
    girl.

Or, possibly the worst transition known to the civilized world:

    The blazing sun MATCH DISSOLVE TO fried egg
    sizzling in pan.

Hmmmm, how can I say this?

DON'T CALL SHOTS!

That's the director's job. No one cares how you would shoot this (except, of course, if you're directing or we're talking about your mother).

At the very beginning of your screenplay, right after FADE IN: is the time when you can describe things very cinematically to set the mood:

    TRAVELING the opening vistas of Texas…

    FLYING OVER the canyons of New York City…

    DOLLYING through the robotic car assembly plant
    in Flint, Michigan…

The other exception is when there's a specific visual you need to highlight an important story point.

```
INT. MONEY COUNTING ROOM — DAY
Munoz sits next to Johnson counting hundreds.

Johnson takes the cigarette dangling out of the
corner of his mouth and stubs it out in the
ashtray.

CLOSE UP of MUNOZ'S HAND
Slipping a stack of hundreds into his pocket.
```

In most cases, if not all cases, you still don't need to actually call the shot. You can write:

```
INT. MONEY COUNTING ROOM — DAY
Munoz sits next to Johnson counting hundreds.

Johnson takes the cigarette dangling out of the
corner of his mouth and stubs it out in the
ashtray.

Munoz slips a stack of hundreds into his pocket.
```

Same result. No calling the shots.

■ EXERCISE 5 — THE LAST WORD ON REMOVING CAMERA SHOTS.

Try rewriting the shots out of these scenes.

```
INT. DIANE'S BATHROOM — NIGHT
TIGHT SHOT of a straight razor glistening on the
white porcelain sink.

MEDIUM SHOT of Diane sitting on the commode, the
tears running down her face. Her trembling hand
picking up the razor.

CLOSE UP of the razor blade slicing through the
tender skin of Diane's wrist.
```

Does your rewrite look something like this?

```
INT. DIANE'S BATHROOM — NIGHT

A straight razor on the white porcelain sink.
```

```
Diane sits on the commode, tears running down
her face.

With her trembling hand she picks up the razor
and slices through the tender skin of her wrist.
```

More efficient writing. Less space taken up — and the director's still talking to you.

camera geography

One of the issues I have with many screenplays I read is the lack of visual logic in scene description.

On some level, we see the movie in our minds when we read it, and when the scene description is illogical or impossible or awkward, it is registered and is one of the things that keep readers from totally being swept away with your writing. Subtle for sure, but real.

When a script is filmed, the director and cameraperson strive to develop shots that move — are cinematic and interesting as they isolate images in the environment.

Screenwriters do the same thing.

How?

By designing the scene description.

If you write a coherent and logical scene description it will never be seen. No one will ever say, "Nice scene description, here's some money." But what it will do is make your seduction of the reader all the smoother, more pleasurable. And that's the goal — to make the read good enough on every level that the reader puts it down feeling positive and wanting to write you a big fat check.

For example:

```
INT. BEDROOM — NIGHT

Diane lies on the bed. On the dresser, black
and white photographs of Diane with Leo. In a
sexy nightgown, Diane sips from a crystal flute
```

of champagne. The moonlight shines through the
window.

                        DIANE
          Leo, you son of a slime bucket!

Okay, not exactly an Oscar-winning scene, I admit that, but
that's not really the point.

Look at the scene description. All the elements are there —
except for the proper camera logic and geography.

Upon analysis, the description is counter to camera logic.
The scene description is not the way the camera would present
the images.

Here's a smoother, more camera-logical version of the same
scene:

    INT. BEDROOM — NIGHT
    The moonlight shines in the window and falls
    across the black and white photographs of
    Dianne and Leo on the dresser then onto Diane,
    in a sexy nightgown, lying on the bed sipping
    champagne out of a crystal flute.

                        DIANE
          Leo, you son of a sludge pump!

This version has another advantage other than being logical
visually. *The description of Diane directly leads into Diane's
dialogue — the best way to do it because the visual of the
character introduces that character's dialogue and makes
for smoother reading.*

I wrote to a student:

**I'd like you to start thinking visually. You need to pay
attention to CAMERA GEOGRAPHY — sometimes
called CAMERA LOGIC — and describe the visuals in a
logical order.**

The student wrote me back:

"I am a little stumped on this. Isn't camera stuff the job of the director? Seeing the scene thru his or her visionary lens? And then the screenwriter's job is the plot, dialogue, story, etc?"

Yes, it is, but your job is to make your script read like a movie because, on some level, we all "see" the movie as we read the script. The more logical visually you write it the better it reads.

There's a logic to what the camera sees. It goes logically from A to B to C to D as the eye would see it. If you go from A to D to C to B — jumping around and not logical. Translate that visually and it's subtly disengaging.

Here's another example:

```
INT. TRAIN — DAY

Sid and David sit opposite each other in the
compartment. Beyond the window pane picturesque
summer meadows, cottages blotched with ivy can
be seen. On the table is a carton of juice and
some fruit. Sid smokes a cigar and David doesn't
like it.
```

Your mind's eye keeps jumping around starting at Sid and David, jumping outside the train, back inside to Sid and David.

See if this is more visually logical:

```
INT. TRAIN — DAY

Beyond the compartment's window pane picturesque
summer meadows, cottages blotched with ivy in
the distance.

A carton of juice and some fruit on the table
between Sid, who is smoking a cigar, and David,
who is leaning away from the smoke.
```

Our mind's eye starts out the train compartment, comes in through the window to the juice on the table then widens to include Sid and David interacting.

■ EXERCISE 6 — THE LAST WORD ON REWRITING FOR VISUAL LOGIC.

Rewrite the scene description below so that is has a visual logic.

```
INT. BEDROOM — NIGHT
The bathroom door opens.
On the bed, Lili is naked, holding a glass of
champagne.
Barefoot, holding his own glass, Senator Snalen,
too naked, walks to her.

Lili LAUGHS.

Outside the wind blows the trees against the
house.

                    LILI
          You're kidding.

                    SNALEN
          What?

                    LILI
          That's what you look like naked?
```

CAPITALIZING

```
The boy WATCHES the kick the can game.

Seehawa hefts the SPEAR and THROWS it.

The lovers KISS.

The BLOOD puddles next to Lois's body.
```

I wrote to the writer:

Please watch your promiscuous capitalizing. All of the above — which I've culled from your script — are incorrect, as are: SUDDENLY, SIDE BY SIDE, SIGNALS, RUSHES.

There are specific rules for capitalization:
   New characters
   Sounds
   Opticals
   Titles
   and that's it.

The reason screenwriters capitalize props (the MANU-SCRIPT, the DIAMOND BRACELET, etc.) derives from how screenwriters prepare a draft for production. Props are capitalized to make sure the Prop Department is aware of the scene's needs.

Don't jump the gun and capitalize in advance of a sale. It makes the read much more difficult because it calls attention to things like SIGNALS and RUSHES that have nothing to do with the story.

character

As I mentioned earlier, one of the few screenwriting rules is TELL STORY THROUGH CHARACTER. CHARACTERS are the way reader/viewers access your script.

Said another way, we enter scripts through the CHARACTERS.

In the best scripts, we're able to go along the journey with the character, experiencing, relating to and empathizing with their experiences. The main character is the PROTAGONIST — the Good Guy.

One of the traditional and proven ways to have reader/viewers hook into a script is to have the main character be PROACTIVE, which means *taking the initiative by acting rather than reacting to events.*

The main character is the motor of your story. He or she gets things done. The protagonist leads the investigation, asks the girl to marry him, breaks into the audition so she can sing for the producer, hunts down the killer, rides the horse in the big race, and de-fuses the nuclear bomb set to blow-up in less than eight seconds.

It is the proactivity of the main character that drives the action of the story.

One of the writers I've been working with is writing a story about a passive, depressed, flat character. It's a tough read because we don't really care about the main character.

I wrote her:

I'd like you to consider giving Charlie fifteen percent more character. I'm not talking angrier, or more sarcastic — not that — but a tad more something that will make the audience root for him a little more and be more fun for the actor to play.

The main character is the emotional heart of your script. It is their emotional roller coaster ride we're on.

The main character usually has a mission, or goal, or a need and we follow along their journey to completion.

the character arc

One of the keys to a successful main character is for him/her to have an arc — where their behavior evolves and changes. Main characters should start in one place — emotionally, psychologically, and in relation to the 'A' story — then move to a new place or places as the movie progresses until they reach their goal or the climax of their journey. As the script moves along the obstacles should be more daunting and the successes sweeter. (*See* RISING ACTION)

A student writes:

"Tom, is it a problem having a main character who is not active, doesn't drive the story?"

It's a problem for me. To have a character who, by definition, is not active, not driving the story, not making the decisions, is a difficult path because it places the main character outside of whatever action you have in the story.

If your story has no story dynamics, you're compounding your problems. You need to think hard about this. In the best of all possible worlds, your character's activity is either driving the story or interacting with the 'A' story throughout.

One of the common mistakes screenwriters make is that their characters blend together; one is not distinguishable from another.

TIPS TO HELP SEPARATE CHARACTERS

1. When you introduce the main characters, describe them visually in a memorable way. The description doesn't have to be lengthy. I once described a character as "A two-hundred dollar haircut and Gucci loafers." The reader gets the picture.

2. Give your character some recognizable and repeatable behavior. Warning: A little of this goes a long way.

3. Your main characters should have different rhythms in their speech — just like real people. Listen to people: they don't speak in perfect sentences. They speak sloppily. Truncated thoughts. That's what makes them and your characters human. Another warning: A little of this goes a long way.

4. Choose character names that aren't similar to other names in your script. (*See* NAMES)

5. Strive for uniqueness in your characters. Not weirdness, but relatable to, memorable traits that intrigue the reader/viewer and want them to learn more.

CREATING MEMORABLE CHARACTERS

The way *not* to create memorable characters is to model your characters on ones you've seen in movies and on television.

The way to do it is to go inside yourself and discover the different facets of the emotional/psychological truths. It is those truths that make screenplays relatable, entertaining and universal in their appeal.

Also, think about the interesting people you know, then combine a couple people's personalities — all true traits — and use those truths to come up with an interesting character.

Scripts where characters have authenticity in their behavior and dialogue are the strongest because they ring true to the reader/viewer. We instinctively reject false emotion and untrue behavior.

Ultimately, I believe all the characters we write, by definition, are parts of us.

Every character, man, woman, alien, penguin, whatever, has been a part of me. I've learned that the deeper I dig within me to reach those universal truths, the better and more memorable my characters are on the page.

MINOR CHARACTERS

I'm reading a student's script — it's good. The main character — a sweet, proactive man — is driving the story. Then he meets up with a colorful young woman. She's a pistol. She's not really vital to the story, yet she dominates the scene with our main character. She's talks rapid fire, is all over the place, funny, nice, sad. It's a three-page scene and she has eighty percent of the dialogue and a hundred percent of the attention.

The scene is seductive because it's good. Fun to read. However, and it's a big however, the scene and the minor character don't sufficiently move the story forward in any tangible way, and she never returns. An amusement yes, but ultimately it damages the script because it takes the reader away from the 'A' story and the main character and doesn't move the story forward. The end result: a negative. Cut it.

Another scene where the minor characters are in the center and our main character is a bystander. Please track through your script any time a minor character arrives on the scene and make sure they're not stealing the movie from the main character.

Too many screenwriters lose control of their script when they introduce their minor characters. I think after writing the main character for so long, the screenwriter finds relief and release in the new characters and they can stretch out and write some new stuff.

Remember, the minor characters are in your script to serve the main story and main characters.

INTRODUCING CHARACTERS

I write to a student:

You should introduce **STANLEY** by name when we first see him playing the video game, instead of just calling him YOUNG BOY. *Whenever you introduce a main character for the first time, you should capitalize their name.* Not necessary for minor characters who don't have dialogue. You should also describe the character the first time we meet them. You want to describe what they look like, what they wear versus what they believe in.

CHARACTER BIOGRAPHIES

One of the writers I worked online with was struggling with his scene list. He wasn't focused on what the movie was he wanted to write. I peppered him with a series of questions — then I didn't hear anything from him.

Two days went by. I pictured him up on a parapet somewhere, eyes wild, tearing his script into pieces and caterwauling to the heavens about screenwriting.

Turns out he was writing. Five days later he surfaced with a revised scene list. And it kicked ass.

I emailed him back.

Good for you for digging deep and pulling this off. Great work. Now, I think it's a good idea to create a CHARACTER BIOGRAPHY for Sam. In fact, figure out who all your main characters are:

> **How did they grow up?**
> **What and who influenced them in their lives?**
> **Where did they go to school?**
> **What was the make-up of their family?**
> **What's their job?**
> **What jobs have they had in the past?**
> **What are their phobias?**
> **How's their health?**

What are their habits, hobbies, flaws, short-comings, strengths, history in relationships and anything else you can think of?

I'm definitely not talking about using this charac-ter biographical information in your script. *The more you know about your characters, the more you'll be informed about how they will behave in the situations you create for them.*

■ EXERCISE 7 – THE LAST WORD ON WRITING YOUR OWN CHARACTER BIOGRAPHY.

Write a Character Biography for yourself. Then take what you've learned and apply those characteristics and insights to your fictional characters.

FILM RECOMMENDATION

Before I leave the subject of character, I'd like to recommend Cindy Meehl's wonderful *Buck*. It's a documentary about a horse trainer, the inspiration for the Robert Redford movie *The Horse Whisperer*. It's a terrific movie because it so wonderfully and subtly presents the complex layers of a man's character. After we finish watching the movie, we understand and respect and care for — and frankly, are a little in awe of — the main char-acter. We're not shown and told everything, but we're given a lot. It's what we're not given, what this movie asks us to put together about this man, that makes it such a masterful presen-tation of character. Definitely worth watching and while you do, think about that fully faceted character as if it weren't a docu-mentary and was a scripted fiction. Pretty good model for the way character can be developed.

clichés

I'm reading along in one of my student's scripts:

```
Clementine was as nervous as a cat in a roomful
of dogs.
```

Another wrote:

```
He shakes her like a rag doll.
```

Another:

```
Warmer than hot buttered rum on a cold day.
```

They keep on coming:

```
He was attracted to her like a moth to flame.
```

What's wrong with these clichés?

Well, firstly, they're clichés.

The reason the script selections don't work? In the first case I'm reading along picturing the movie I'm reading — when suddenly, in the middle of this caper movie, I see a cat in a roomful of dogs.

And in the next I see the ragdoll.

And a mug of hot buttered rum.

And finally, a moth burning horribly to death in the flame of a candle.

The point is none of these images appear in the movies — they appear in the writing. And that's counter-productive because it takes the reader out of the scripts. (*See* METAPHORS AND SIMILES)

When I was writing television for über-producer Steve Cannell (I wrote staff for *Hunter* and *Stingray* for a couple of years), he would red-pencil every single cliché any writer wrote in a script. I argued that that's the way people spoke. I lost because his name was on the building and that's the way he wanted it. I'm not sure if it's a black or white issue. Sometimes a cliché is appropriate.

VISUAL CLICHÉS

Fast motion of crowds in the big city — **Seen it a million times.**
  Slow motion violence — **How many times have we seen that?**
  Slow motion to highlight something — **Old hat.**

One of many notes I wrote to this writer about his gimmicky, distracting slo-mo heavy script:

The super slow motion of the bullet spinning toward its target is so cliché that, at this point, it reads like a joke or that you're writing a parody.

The idea isn't to try to write visuals you've seen in other movies: you want your script to be original, to feel fresh, not something the reader has seen before — on any level.

coincidences and accidents

Rebecca, one of my online writers, submitted pages that were filled with convenient story elements. I wrote her:

Rebecca, the key moments in your story turn out to be coincidences: Wolf stumbles over the keys to the Rolls Royce; he knocks over a vase, which breaks, revealing the map conveniently hidden inside; he trips and falls into the door revealing Dr. Fuentes' secret lab. It's not satisfying that Wolf doesn't do anything other than stumble and be clumsy and that the big clues in the movie come so easily to him. Work harder. Make Wolf earn it.

And to another writer:

Not sure about the accidental story moment where the hidden checkbook falls from the car visor moving the story along. It's like the hand of the writer reaching in from out of frame and handing her the checkbook.

More notes:

Again, I think the storytelling is too easy. Jose stumbles coincidently over Annie's bag, then six pages later, he stumbles coincidently over a VIDEO CAMERA. Too many coincidental stumbles.

Even more:

Jose figures out what the plot is — but he sure hasn't worked hard to do it. One of the real issues in this

script is the lack of investigatory success for Jose. He's on the run a lot — but there are so many coincidences, things just falling into our hero's lap. It's not terribly satisfying.

The answer is to keep your main character proactive. (*See* MAIN CHARACTERS)

computers, phone calls, letters

Stephen opens the letter. His loan has been
denied.

**Norma, can Stephen get this bad news in person, say
at the bank, so you can have dialogue and a real scene
with real people versus a scene with a piece of paper?
It's a real important moment in your story. To communicate this vital information in a letter — no matter
how real — seems to diminish the drama. You should be
trying to maximize rather than minimize it.**

Leonid receives an email informing him that the
British have charged him with war crimes.

**This is the single most dramatic moment in your script
so far and Leonid gets the bad news by email. How
about a messenger from the government? How about
a government official? How about from his wife? My
suggestion is to write a few different versions of the
scene and see how they play.**

Miranda overhears that the Japanese have invaded
Pearl Harbor.

**Miranda's on the outside of the action, overhear-
ing it. Why not have the father, who now returns later
in the day, come home now and tell Miranda and the
others directly?**

And finally:

Larry picks up the phone.

                    RITA
        Hey

                    LARRY
        I'm so glad you called. What are you
        doing tonight?

                    RITA
        I'm leaving you.

                    LARRY
                (panicked)
        Rita!

    CLICK. Larry can't believe it.

I couldn't either.

Was there no other way to play this?

Would it have been more effective in person, with accompanying drink thrown in face (talk about clichés) or a fork in the eye? (that's better) Look through your script and make sure you're making these moments as dramatic as they should be.

Look for devices like phone calls, letters and computers that isolate characters and distance them from the drama. Try to write actual dramatic face-to-face scenes and see if they work any better.

Check to see that you've found the most dramatic way to tell your story that involves characters talking, feeling and behaving. The more dramatic those big story moments are, the better your movie.

We all spend lots and lots of time on the phone, on our computers, on our iPads, and iPods and iWhatnots, but let me tell you: that's not the stuff of movies. People on computers are boring. People on the phone are boring. There's nothing like human contact.

That being said, *The Social Network*, as you know one of my favorite movies in recent years, has lots of computer scenes. They're fast and visual and right on the 'A' story — and they work.

PHONE CALL FORMATTING
One of my Russian students asked me to show her how to write phone calls. I showed her a few different ways:

BOTH SIDES OF THE CALL:

```
INT. TOM'S OFFICE — DAY
Tom dials his cell phone.

EXT. MOSCOW — NIGHT (INTERCUT WHEN NEEDED)
Violetta hears her phone RING and pulls it out
of her purse.

                    VIOLETTA
          Hello?

                    TOM
          Hi, it's Tom.

                    VIOLETTA
          I told you stop calling me.
```

ONE SIDE OF THE CONVERSATION:

```
EXT. MOSCOW — NIGHT
Violetta answers her cell phone.

                    VIOLETTA
          Hello.

                    TOM'S VOICE
                 (over phone)
          Hi, it's Tom.

                    VIOLETTA
          If you call me again, I'll call the
          Police.
```

Because phones and PDAs are so prevalent, it's hard to imagine the contemporary landscape without them. When I see eighty percent of the people in the street holding their cell phones, even if not looking at them or texting, I think that's the way I should write everyone these days, but, frankly, I don't. A few of my characters obsessively carry their cell phones. It's the screenwriter's call.

common screenwriting misteaks

In each of the examples cited below, the professional reader recognizes these extremely common mistakes and they're pulled out of the script. That's the last thing you want. Most of these mistakes are covered in other places in this book, but I'm hoping readers will cut this page from the book and post it near their computers or tape it to their foreheads, whichever works better.

In my experience, writers make many of the same mistakes in every script they write. Let this chapter serve as a quick reference and reminder.

WE SEE, WE HEAR, WE FOLLOW, WE ANYTHING

It's a given that everything on the screen is heard and seen. The use of WE as a literary form is also redundant. You don't have to tell the reader they're the reader or there is a reader/viewer. WE FOLLOW is the calling of a camera shot, which, as you know, is not your job.

CUT TO:

Unneeded. Old school. Again, it states the obvious. There is, by definition, a cut between every scene. *Skip an extra line between scenes and that will make your script easier to read.*

CLOSE UP, WIDE SHOT, MATCH CUT, PAN TO

Any calling of shots is *verboten*. Maybe if I say it in German you'll listen.

WRITE THE TOUGH SCENES
(*See* SCENES YOU DON'T WRITE)

EVERY SLUG LINE NEEDS A SCENE DESCRIPTION UNDER IT

A maddeningly common mistake. Every time there is no scene description under a slug line — which is read as a mistake — it pulls the reader out of the script. (*See* ARMY TAKES THE TOWN for reasons you have to have scene description)

ETC. AND SO ON

Don't leave it for your readers to fill in the blanks. It's your job to fully describe what is going on. Look at it as an opportunity to better sell your script. Take responsibility for what you're presenting. Using "etc." is not an option.

THE FIRST LETTER OF ALL PRODUCTS IS CAPITALIZED

Coke, Corvette, The Wall Street Journal. (*See* CAPITALIZING)

MONTAGES

distance the reader from the material. They work great on film, not so much in screenplays. (*See* MONTAGES)

WHEN THE SAME CHARACTER HAS CONSECUTIVE DIALOGUE BOXES, THE SECOND NEEDS A (CONT'D)

When we read your script we don't pay attention to format issues until they jump out at us. We're used to reading dialogue going from character to character unless there's a (CONT'D) under the character name signaling the same character is speaking again. When you violate this rule, the reader is taken out of your script. For just a split second. It may not seem important to you, but add up a series of these little indiscretions and it makes a difference. Your script should be perfect so your work can be judged on its merits, not this little, poopy stuff. The cliché is something about "Don't lose the coat for the buttons."

WEIGHT YOUR WRITING

Write important parts with more detail than the unimportant parts so the reader can sense which is the most important. (*See* WEIGHTING YOUR WRITING)

MISCELLANEOUS MISTAKES

Every slug line needs a time reference — DAY, NIGHT, DUSK, MORNING.

Everything we read on screen — newspaper headlines, names on doors, notes, letters, emails — needs to be underlined.

SIMILES AND METAPHORS DON'T WORK in screenplays as they conjure up images in the mind of the reader that aren't in the movie. (*See* METAPHORS AND SIMILES)

EVERY QUESTION NEEDS A QUESTION MARK

I know I'm reading like a fussbudget anal-compulsive twerpy kind of a nerdazoid, but you really do want your script to have the best chance it can have. That's what it's about. No regrets.

WHEN YOU GO TO ANOTHER ROOM IT'S A NEW SCENE — WITH ITS OWN SLUG LINE (EXT. YARD — DAY)

When not done, a sure sign of an amateur.

CHARACTER DESCRIPTION WORDING

```
Moira, a beautiful redhead, enters the ballroom.

Andy, a six-foot hunk, strips off his shirt.

Kelly, dressed in a nightgown, limps up the
stairs.
```

It's boring to read the same sentence structure each and every time you describe a character.

Change it up a bit, like...

```
Dressed in a nightgown, Kelly limps…
```

■ EXERCISE 8 – THE LAST WORD ON WRITING CHARACTER DESCRIPTION.

Try experimenting with character description. Write the description of a main character you've written about or are writing about. After you have the description written, examine it. Is it a cliché? Can you make it more unique to this character? Now rewrite it again, examine once more, then rewrite it one last time.

communicating
what you want to

> As the sirens shriek outside, Clive, in a daze, puts on his clothes and walks into the hall.
>
> There is chaos and officers running around.
>
> "It's war! It's war!"
>
> Clive gets into the break room/office/main room, and everyone is literally screaming like hell.
>
> Across the room, he sees a fresh pot of coffee — a small island of order — pours himself a cup.

I wrote the writer:

Brent, ignoring all the many format issues for the moment, this is our main character. While there's chaos around him as the world explodes into war — our hero couldn't care less and fixes himself a cup of coffee. Not the way heroes act. Please reconsider this.

The writer wrote me:

"He's still trying to digest everything amidst all the madness, so that's why he drinks coffee, to slowly make sense out of everything. I mean, he's looking around observing everyone while doing this, absorbing. He's not being passive. At least that's what I feel. Isn't it normal or essential for people to drink coffee in the morning in order to function? Let me know what you think on this."

Brent, it doesn't play that way. Our hero should be in action when there's a crisis. He has to transcend not

being a morning person and being able to function in an emergency

And as for it being normal or essential for people to drink coffee in order to function? It's the beginning of a World War!!! My guess is his adrenaline would kick in and he would function at the top of his capability without a hot cup of Joe.

crank it up!

A student from Australia was writing a script about islanders experiencing a monster hurricane. Even as the hurricane winds are whipping over the island, our heroes are lollygagging around finishing a game of croquet.

I wrote her:

Renata, where's the sense of urgency? Your main characters are so laid back when the hurricane is roaring toward them, knocking down palm trees, flooding the lowlands. Shouldn't they be running for their lives? The clock should be ticking. You have to crank up their reaction to the impending disaster. This is the moment. Write it!

Another writer was writing a horror movie, but he wasn't delivering the horror. Too tame. And in horror, too tame is not good.

I think you're right on track in terms of beginning your story. Take another pass. Don't censor anything. Try and push yourself to go beyond your comfort zone. Take more chances. Bigger, stranger, more rituals, more ooga booga, more scares, more surprises. You're selling horror with this script. Sell it! Crank it up!

A writer I was working with was writing a small, personal story. And it was pretty damn good. But the script was too small and too personal and I was worried that no one would

THE LAST WORD ■ LAZARUS

care because the people and incidents were so limited and non-demonstrative — and if we don't get in, we move on.

I wrote the writer:

This is a really good beginning. But, it's very slight and doesn't have much of a narrative pull. You should focus your rewrite on using the same good writing and excellent observation and see if you can ramp up the story to something we have a stake in. Crank it up!

Another writer was writing flat. No story or character elements were sold at all — just presented. It wasn't bad, but everything just lay on the page like a dead mackerel. The script had no life. No Hollywood. No movie.

Yes, I wanted you to see that fish in the middle of my writing.

I wrote the writer:

Your script has to be glamorized, visualized, maximized. The drama has to be more dramatic, the betrayals bigger, the twists and turns more extreme.

And, who's the bad guy? Before doing anything else, I'd like you to rewrite these pages and crank up the emotions. Leslie never talks to anyone about her loss. About anything. I think all the human behavior is a little too tight, a little to — to use a cliché — close to the vest. Crank it up!

default position as a writer

One of my on-site writers always made the same mistake. He would tell the reader what was going to happen or was happening in the scene, then the characters would do the scene.

I wrote him:

Your job as a screenwriter is to try and figure out what it is you continue to do that is not good for your script. In your case, one of your default positions is to tell the reader what the scene is versus let the scene play out.

Once you discover what your built-in weaknesses are, then you should take special pains to be on the lookout for them. I would dedicate one rewrite solely to eliminating any of the default writing.

My default writing position is not having my characters' emotions go far enough in my scripts. It's something I'm very diligent about now, but end up having to deal with my characters less-than emotional levels in every script I write.

■ EXERCISE 9 – THE LAST WORD ON DISCOVERING YOUR WRITING FLAWS.

Examine your own writing. Think about the notes you've been given. Is there a common thread? Is there some mistake you keep making over and over? See if you can write a DEFAULT POSITIONS document for yourself listing the continuing issues you should be aware of in your writing.

description

A script I was reading was dialogue-centric. I couldn't see the movie at all.

I wrote to the writer:

I have no idea what this movie looks like, what the houses, rooms, backyards look like, what the characters are wearing. *Your job as a screenwriter is to report what we see on the screen.* **YOU NEED TO DO THIS. Right now, it's all dialogue — a radio show. Just voices. You're asking each reader to invent their own visuals. Not a good idea. Take responsibility.**

Another writer wrote description — but too much:

```
EXT. WESTPORT — DAY
A small stream of water trickles on the street,
next to the curb.

It's coming from the gravel driveway next door,
where the neighbor's adolescent daughter washes
her white four-door SUV.

Her name is LORETTA SIMONS, 17, red hair and
sassy. Tanned legs extend from her shorts, an
almost transparent tank top clings to her pouty
breasts. She's smoking hot and draws attention
to her red lips by smacking on a lollipop.

Bill and Karen come out of the front door. Walk
towards the shiny red sports car, parked in the
driveway, facing out, ready to go. The vanity
license…
```

Wait a minute. Wait a minute. We don't need to know all this. What's important here?

Because this is near the beginning of your script, I'm afraid the reader's heart will sink at the prospect of reading a whole script with such dense description — particularly when it's not important. (*See* WEIGHTING YOUR WRITING)

If Loretta's important, why begin with the trickle of water? When the movie is shot, the cinematographer may come up with an extraordinary shot based on what he sees through the camera, but until then, let the filmmakers know what you, as the screenwriter, deem important in the scene by how you write it.

■ EXERCISE 10 – THE LAST WORD ON CUTTING DOWN DESCRIPTION.

Cut the above description down to the bare essentials — probably leaving out "pouty."

I think you'll be shocked how much you can weed out and still communicate what's important. The trick is to make it concise and still leave some of the colorful imagery.

Too much description slows the script down:

```
A lady with thick glasses and an enormous
overbite is close behind. A ghastly orange-
hued home hair dye job gone bad, a long purple
flowery dress and purple shoes. She nibbles
on candies from a purple fuzzy teddy bear PEZ
dispenser. This is JUDY, 50, who just might be
the owner.
```

"Enormous overbite?" A description of a minor character's dental characteristics?

Do we need to know that the "dye job has gone bad"?

"Purple fuzzy teddy bear PEZ dispenser"?

For a minor prop in a minor scene with minor characters to carry this level of description is over the top — to say the least.

The idea is to get a flow with your writing so the reader is just taken away — not to stop the forward momentum by this kind of ponderously colorful description.

When you minimize writing in unimportant areas and write more specifically in important areas it cues the reader as to what's important. (See WEIGHTING YOUR WRITING)

The reader invests in a long passage and when it doesn't resonate in the screenplay they're wary about trusting the writer again.

Another writer sent me this:

```
Mugsy rides his motorcycle into the trailer
park and climbs off it in front of Weinberg's
trailer.
```

I don't have a sense of what the trailer park looks like? Upscale? Cheesy? Desert? Woods? Is Mugsy wearing shorts and work boots? Jeans? Flip flops? And the motorcycle? The trailer? Help the reader see your movie.

```
A cityscape of unbridled capitalism.
```

You should be describing what's on the screen — not the rampant financial activity which tells about the fiscal aspects of the city but doesn't physically describe what it looks like — and that's your job.

```
Lyman dances with the fluidity of someone in a
full body-cast.
```

Funny, but, unfortunately, not in the movie.

Shane Black, big-time Hollywood writer, made a huge splash a number of years ago. His writing was characterized by smart-ass remarks he, the writer, made directly to the reader. He made tons of money and a wave of screenwriting, with clever notes to the reader, suddenly was all that I was reading. It's never appropriate and is, at least in my mind, way too needy a strategy for a screenwriter to employ. For me, it's way too much "Love me, please love me." I think the writer should trust what he or she is writing and let what's on the screen carry it.

I recently saw Mr. Black's directorial effort *Kiss Kiss Bang Bang* and those now legend smart-ass voice overs directed right to the viewer made it into the film — and totally ruined the flow of the movie. To me it violated one of the foundations of screenwriting: don't let the reader pull out of your script — the smart-ass comments are a parallel reality and have no place in a screenplay.

I should only have a little of Shane Black's success.

dialogue

One of my students submitted a sorority thriller. You know, screaming coeds in tight sweaters running from zombies. I love those scripts. Unfortunately, it didn't work because the kids didn't sound authentic. They sounded like young people at a meeting of Mensa.

> **Mickey — these kids don't talk like college kids. They use words like "eschew" and "I don't deign," and phrases like "I'm still ruminating" and "Don't get all sacrosanct up in my face."**

Danny, a college kid, the son of a close friend, recently emailed his father and told him about a test he'd just taken: "Made that test my bitch! Fuck yah!" Sounds like a kid to me.

ADDITIONAL THOUGHTS ON DIALOGUE:

Dialogue is totally different than the written word. It's to be heard — not read.

Say your dialogue out loud. See if it's comfortable in your mouth and can be said easily. Particularly, see how it sounds, if it has the natural halting rhythms of speech and feels right in your ear.

Have someone, preferably actors, read your script to you so you can hear it. That's what it's about. Listen to how they speak your lines.

Listen to real people talking: on buses, in elevators, standing on line, in doctor's offices. Listen to the rhythms, the hesitations, the pauses, the repeated words, the incomplete sentences.

Write down what you hear, so you can see what it looks like as the written word. Sometimes you'll overhear a great line that you can save for the right character in the right scene.

Make your dialogue not be too "on the nose" — obvious and exactly what the character means.

Short dialogue blocks are good.

Long speeches or speechifying is not good.

Your ear is the last word for dialogue. If it sounds authentic, that's your goal.

disclosure of
information

One of my onsite writers was writing a police procedural and it wasn't working.

> **You have to figure out when we know things and when Lars (the main character) does. There's no need for us to know before Lars. If we do, we're just waiting for him to catch up. Not a good thing.**

And to another writer:

> **Not sure we want to see the tattoo yet. You have to plot out very carefully when we know things and when Juno does. There's no need for us to know before Juno.**

Sound familiar? How about this one?

> **When does Jayne find out her teacher's name is Edward? Surely, she's seen his name on school material — bulletin boards, report cards. When do we find out? This misunderstanding is one of the cornerstones of your script so you've got to make the facts in here crystal clear and rock hard consistent.**

My suggestion is to graph out — in a scene list — the exact moments in your script where you disclose important information to the reader/viewer. In that way, you'll be in control of the information and disseminate it at the proper time for the maximum effect.

My bias, as you've no doubt gathered, is to have the reader/viewer play along with the main character in terms of what he or she knows. *It's more fun to play along than to observe.* (*See* WRITING A PAGE-TURNER)

Some screenwriters have a tendency to "Spill the beans" or have characters run off at the mouth telling who they are and setting everything up.

Here are my notes to one such writer:

You're giving away so much of what Laura's job should be — getting to the bottom of what's going on here, then she has a scene with George and just runs off at the mouth again and everything we'll ever want to know about her comes out. Don't be so promiscuous with the information. Plot how you disclose it and where.

The idea is to spread the information out so there is always more the reader wants to learn — rather than giving it to them all at one time.

The same is true with your Hiram character. He tells the reader in that clunky exposition with his brother much more than Laura knows — so we have to wait until Laura catches up with what we know. The rule is: *We don't want the reader/viewer ahead of the main character*. We want to play along with the protagonist, experience what she's experiencing.

A writer was writing a detective story and was taking, rather than the Detective's POV, a more universal presentation of the story. *An open story.* So, we knew who the criminal was. We saw him in the dreaded opening bookends scene. (*See* OPEN STORY VS. CLOSED STORY)

Why are you spending so much time with Kemal and the police?

We, the audience, know he didn't do it. You showed us who did it already. So, these scenes have no value for us and we end up treading water. Either lose the opening so we don't know Kemal didn't do it or cut the scene.

A little bit further in the script:
This is another scene following the investigation of Kemal and Bob as suspects, when we, the audience, *still* know neither of them did it. Makes us more and more impatient. The reader is losing faith in you as the writer.

To another writer I wrote:
These pages feel so on-the-nose, so expositiony, if there is such a word. Your characters are telling us exactly what they think. Consider holding off the specific information and the letters and make the scene about her hatred of the University. Let us find out later — with her — about the letters. Arc both the information as well as the story.

GRATUITOUS INFORMATION

Around page thirty in this writer's script, Henderson, the bad guy, arrives on the scene, and twirling his mustache, explains the details of his plot against the townspeople.

Why would he do that? What does he have to gain giving away his game plan? And just as importantly, no one asked him.

I'm always concerned when the bad guy explains the essence of his plan in great detail. Too easy. In the best of all possible worlds, the hero should discover and piece together the plan. That's what makes him or her a hero.

A few pages further, more notes:
I'm getting impatient for something to happen. So far what are we dealing with? A woman who lives in a parallel universe and whose present existence consists of moving into a new condo, having breakfast with the family next door and talking to her mother on the

phone for three pages! No drama. No conflict. Just a few asides about being from another universe. It's never dealt with directly and we're almost halfway through the script. I can't help but feel the opening pages of the script are way, way too slow.

dreams

```
INT. RANDY'S BEDROOM — MORNING
Randy springs from bed and runs out of the
bedroom.

INT. LIVING ROOM — CONTINUOUS
Felix is standing in front of the window. He is
dressed in the finest clothes money can buy.

                    FELIX
         Randy, my boy, come over here and
         give your Father a hug!

Randy runs to Felix, goes to hug him, but Felix
disappears!

INT. A TINY BEDROOM — MORNING
Randy wakes with a start. Sweat is on his brow.
```

What? You mean after seventy pages Randy finally finding his father was only a dream? Well, I'm not sure that works. After all I've been through with Randy for him to finally find his father, and then for me, the poor schlump reader, to find out I've been tricked. Let's talk about this.

That Randy never found his father, well, I felt used and dirty. Maybe not that bad, but more negative than positive. The issue with dreams for me is that many times they're the most dramatic and creative part of the script — and the rest of the script pales in comparison. Not such a good thing because usually dreams are only a very small percentage of the page count and that leads us to have expectations that are unrealized.

Then another note a bunch of pages later:

Why a dream here? Why give away that Felix is gone before Randy and we can experience it. It vitiates the drama. It gives away the story. Those are the negatives for running a dream sequence. And the positives? Frankly, I can't think of any.

Dreams are questionable at any time, but to open your movie with a dream is particularly odious. What happens at the beginning of your script is that the reader is one hundred percent with you. Totally committed to reading. Open to everything. After a page they surrender and begin to be swept away. Then, a few scenes later or a few pages later, the main character wakes up — it's all been a dream!

When that happens?

The readers feel tricked. Duped. What a rip off. Their investment has been for naught. They've been had. And they begin feeling something other than positive feelings for the script and the writer. And they've just started reading.

If the script-making-me-feel-bad happens too often to me — I start searching for the screenwriter's address so I can hunt him or her down — just sayin'.

The point is: it can't be a good idea to alienate your reader in the first few pages. That's the risk you take opening your script with a dream. Is it worth the risk?

Keep these thoughts in mind when you use a dream:

Make sure your dreams are necessary.

Make sure they move the story forward.

Make sure they're not the most creative or exciting thing in your script.

Martin Scorsese, a filmmaker I really admire, had in his fascinating movie *Hugo* this sequence of scenes:

```
A frantic chase.
Our young hero almost gets caught.
```

```
He wakes up.
It was a dream.
But now the villain is really after him.
The hero almost gets caught again.
And he wakes up again. Another dream.
```

Back-to-back dream sequences!

Do Scorsese's back-to-back dream sequences work?

Yes.

Do I recommend you do it?

No.

endings

This was the ending to a writer's script:

```
EXT. BOARDWALK — SUNSET
Flo and Seymour walk along near the railing
noticing all the details around them.

They sit on one of the wooden benches and take
each other's hand.

                                     FADE OUT

          The End
```

Huh? Is that the end? What do you want us to feel? What are Flo and Seymour feeling? I don't think it's clear enough what your intentions are. Dig deeper. Write more. Be more explicit.

And another writer's ending.

```
Paula looks at Lydia. Neither speaks. Neither
knows what to say.

               FADE OUT

          The End
```

I don't know what to say either. This ending isn't satisfying. I've spent a hundred and six pages following Paula and Lydia's stories, through thick and thin, and now the movie just ends. No climax? No epiphany? No nothing. It just dribbles to an end without them knowing what to say?

If they had something to say, what would it be?

I'd like to see you go back and re-think the ending and see if you can build to a climax where Paula or Lydia, or both of them, end their stories in a satisfying way.

Here's a script note to another writer:
Upon reaching the end, I feel there's not enough story — not enough twists — not enough turns. But the big issue for me is that Joe doesn't learn anything. He's in the exact place he was at the beginning of the script. He hasn't grown. Think about other possible endings, of Joe being happy with Tawny or something that isn't a downer.

Step back, re-scene list your script. Think about other possibilities.

Thinking about writing counts as writing.

After finishing reading a script, I find myself asking writer after writer: **"What do you want us to feel at the end your script?"**

It's such an important question. If the reader feels satisfied, if character arcs work and story threads are resolved — happy ending or not — you've done your job.

If the read is good — easy, exciting, full — and the time spent with your script is a positive experience, it opens the door to a sale.

A script that grabs the reader by the throat and never lets the reader out of its grip is the best kind of script you can write.

Something else about endings: About twenty pages or so before FADE OUT — it varies in every script — your story should start "running for the barn" — using the horseback riding metaphor referencing horses, who once they sense they're heading home, start racing for the barn. Your script should build, get more exciting, faster, more urgent, then climax to a FADE OUT.

I'M HAVING TROUBLE FINDING MY ENDING

Discouraged that she couldn't find her ending and had stopped writing, the screenwriter wrote me for help.

"Dear Tom –

I was going along just fine, I really was, I'm almost half-way through my scene list, but I can't seem to come up with an ending that seems right. I stopped writing because I really don't know where this script is going. Can you help me?"

My script note:

I wouldn't let not having an ending slow you down in any way. Go through your scene list again — from the beginning — adding whatever seems right. When you reach the end, hopefully fueled by new scenes and new insights, give the ending another try.

Here's something else to try: make a list of possible endings. Spend some time brainstorming. It counts as writing. Don't reject anything. Keep trying things. Free associate. Let your mind float. This also counts as writing. See where it goes. Be patient. It will come together. Remember it's a process. No matter what: Keep writing!

establishing scenes

The opening shot of a script:

```
EXT. THE DESERT — SUNSET
Long shadows from the cactus stretch across the
vast, barren landscape. FOOTSTEPS. The heavy
boots of RANGER slog through the deep sand.
```

Your descriptive desert shot establishes the main location of the movie, a sense of what the movie looks like and hopefully a little of the mood. I like it.

In the middle of scripts, establishing shots help give your script some air, a time for breathing between scenes — a rest — as well as the general, visual introduction to a new location.

To a student:

How about an establishing shot of the lake? This is now the third establishing shot I've suggested. I think I'm looking to get a little more "movie" into the script. Take more advantage of your interesting locations.

Another screenwriter wrote:

```
EXT. HOTEL — DAY
Establishing shot. The hotel stands proudly in
the mid-day sun.
```

My script note:

You don't need to tell the reader that it's an establishing shot. It *is* an establishing shot, by definition. Just let it be.

Plus, try not to have a scene that just establishes the hotel. Find some content to combine with the establishing shot — preferably with our main character in it — so you can establish and move the story forward at the same time.

We'll get the kind of things you want to establish in your establishing scene as background and the foreground will be richer with content.

And finally:

Consider putting in an EXT. TRAIN STATION scene — everyone loves steam engines and it'll give the picture some more interesting visuals and a snapshot of society — before you go INT. TRAIN — DAY.

■ EXERCISE 11 – THE LAST WORD ON ESTABLISHING SHOTS.

Go through your script and before you move to any new location analyze to see if an Establishing Shot is needed to allow some air and space into your script or not.

every scene must move the story forward

A note to one of my students:

As good as your scene of the kid singing is — how does it move the story forward? The answer is it doesn't. That means you're going to have to lose it.

I've spent a lot of time in the editing room cutting footage into television shows and movies. The usual procedure is you have to deliver, let's say, a ninety-minute movie and your rough cut is a hundred and ten minutes long. Twenty minutes of footage needs to be cut. Cut my footage? Are you kidding? Every word I wrote and every foot I shot is gold, pure gold.

My enormous ego aside, what makes this difficult editorial process easier is one of the few rules that work in the shaping of movies as well as scripts: *EVERY SCENE MUST MOVE THE STORY FORWARD.*

I can't say it enough: **EVERY SCENE MUST MOVE THE STORY FORWARD!**

The way to evaluate that is to take the scene out of your scene list or script or rough cut and if it doesn't impact the 'A' story in a negative way — that should tell you the scene is unneeded.

There's a not particularly pleasant expression — children please turn away — "Eating your babies." That means your beloved babies — those scenes and characters you just love — if they don't move the story forward — they have to go. It's hard to be ruthless, but you have to be.

If you learn only one thing from this book:

**EVERY SCENE MUST
MOVE THE STORY FORWARD!**

exposition

I'm twenty pages into a script and it's tough going.

My note to the writer:

I've just been told a whole bunch of things about who Lance is, his dreams, what he wants, what his parents want for him, told a lot things and it's pretty slow going. Nothing particularly insightful or important, just setting up the characters and what they do and think — pretty standard stuff — no surprises. Lots of telling rather than showing.

Okay, save your pages, then go through these twenty pages and pull out the exposition. You have so much and you need so little. Trust the story we're watching. The less you tell us the more we're engaged. Now read the rewritten pages. If they're better, move on. If they're not, restore the original pages.

The writer made the cuts, liked ninety percent of them and moved on.

Exposition explains backstory and presents information the author thinks is needed to fully understand what's going on.

Well, my issue is the term "Fully understand." I don't think it's such a good idea to fully understand. Keep giving the reader just the exposition that's absolutely necessary, but don't give them all the information. Keep them guessing. Keep them involved. Let the reader/viewer work a little. It's what keeps them engaged.

When writers I'm working with are starting a new script, I tell them not to write any exposition. Most of the time it's excess baggage and just slows the script down. If after writing a draft without exposition you feel you need to put some in — fine.

We're such sophisticated readers and viewers that we just don't need to know every little thing about what has happened in the past. It's better for the reader/viewer to be actively engaged in the story trying to figure things out rather than having all the information spoon fed to them.

If you feel that exposition is absolutely necessary — and sometimes I do get that it is — do your best to hide it. *Hide the exposition in a fight, sprinkled in an action scene or in an argument.* The idea is to make sure your characters have florid enough attitudes that the exposition doesn't seem to be exposition.

fix it now

I was working with a writer/director in a couple of my UCLA classes and I kept giving him the note to get his main character into the center of the script, which was really good. Ultimately, he never really did it. Two years later he got the script made with Sally Field, which was a great accomplishment. One of the problems with the movie was that the main character wasn't in the center of the movie.

It's no surprise that what was wrong with the script is what's wrong with the movie. My advice: fix it now while you can.

flashbacks

On page 104 of a writer's 110-page script the writer ran a three-page flashback of the two main characters ten years earlier in an emotional scene. It froze the script in place and ruined the otherwise good ending.

I think the extended flashback of Liam and Lacy is absolutely unneeded. It stops your momentum — right near the end — and brings your script to a dead stop. If you have to prove or explain their relationship at this point, then you're in big trouble. Try it without the flashback and you'll see it doesn't make any difference. So lose it so you don't interrupt your build to your ending.

Following is a conversation I had with another writer.
Just as your script is beginning to pick up momentum, you throw in another of those damned flashbacks and all of your forward movement grinds to a halt. And now, ten pages later, another flashback. You're sabotaging this script by not letting the forward momentum gather. You keep stopping the momentum by flashback and exposition and memories — KEEP MOVING FORWARD!

The writer wrote me back:
"The flashback is necessary to show the status-quo of the main character and show that he lost his daughter early in the story."

No it isn't. It's backstory. Not necessary at all.

"Later we will see how he can overcome his past."
We'll still get that even if we don't see the flashback.

"This conversation tells us about the character of Allie even before we see her for the first time."
That's exactly what's wrong with it. It tells us something when it's better for us to experience it the first time.

"We get to know that Allie really wants to follow her father's wake and fights with her uncle over her career choice. That's her motive for starting her adventure and that's what we NEED to see early on the story."
No we don't. We need to see that when it happens in the story — not in advance. My advice is to tell your story of Allan and his daughters' big adventure and have exposition when you need it — not before the fact.

"It's really hard not to agree with that statement. I'll keep this in mind. At the same I believe that I prove that the flashback scene and talk between Allan and his ex-wife is necessary early in the story."
It's not. The flashbacks take us out of the script and become a piece of writing. The flashbacks don't change anything. Don't move the story forward and don't work. Trust your story and characters. (*See* SPLINTERING TIME)

FOLLOW-UP: The writer never made the changes. He now lives in a five-million-dollar mansion in Beverly Hills. When taking his exposition-heavy script to the post office to send out, he was hit by a Paramount Pictures truck and received a huge settlement.

format

I make a big deal about format because it's the most fixable of script problems. It's not a judgment call. It's simple. Correct format is a given. Any deviation takes the reader out of your script. That's the deal.

To save space and speed things along, this screenwriter did away with the normal slug lines. She listed the scenes:

```
MONTAGE BEGINS
1. Wong drives a tractor through town.
2. Wong dances in front of the church fathers.
3. Wong opens a beer and chugs the whole can.
4. Wong swims in the big pool.
```

And it went on and on for eleven scenes. No slug lines with locations and Day or Night. No descriptions. No dialogue. No music. No selling the concept of the scenes. No details for us to hook into. Just a flat list of scenes. No taking responsibility. Wrong.

My script note:

You've abandoned proper format for expediency. A professional reader gets what you're doing (saving space) and becomes annoyed at what can be construed as mistakes. I think you lose more credibility and professionalism than you gain in space. Formatting is vital in selling the professionalism of the screenwriter.

(Please see MONTAGES *for more reasons not to write montages)*

DEVIATING FROM FORMAT

One of my long-time students submitted a script where he made a number of absolutely misguided format choices that I felt severely damaged his script.

Not only did he pre-lap dialogue (running dialogue from an incoming scene over the end of the outgoing scene) but he pre-lapped images — something I'd never seen before and hope never to see again.

I was distressed and wrote him.

The whole point I'm trying to make about your script is that all the audio and visual pre-lap deviates from "normal" format, taking the reader out of the script to deal with the format aberration. That "taking the reader out of your script" is, obviously, a bad thing and not worth whatever you get by including these format miscues.

The seasoned reader, like producers and contest judges, are all pros and the last thing you want is for them to have a similar reaction to mine.

He didn't agree. His defense and the reason he made these choices was that he'd seen pre-laps done by "Working professionals, good ones at that," he said, and therefore he figured it was okay.

I wrote him back:

No matter how right you are and how many other scripts you've seen pre-lapping work in, I don't think the upside is worth it.

As a matter of fact, the real-world decision on all of these transitions that you've so carefully fashioned will be made in the editing room. So the issue is only how it works in the script and, in my mind, there's more damage being done including these aberrations than any benefits to your script.

My guess is he probably left them. (*For more on formatting please see* THE SCENE)

A note about what you read in scripts by professionals — and good ones at that. Anything written by a seasoned pro with a proven track record will be taken positively because of the writer's reputation. And it's probably a pretty good read.

For a writer without a reputation, any aberrant formatting will most likely be read as negative. Any script that creates doubt is not something a reader will pass onto a producer.

for god's sake, hurry!

My notes to a consultation:

> **So much talk. So little action. Why do we care? Five pages in the car is way too much — just dialogue. Too leisurely. Too slow. If I wasn't being paid, I would have put the script down on page 23.**

> **They arrive at the gas station and it takes two minutes of dialogue before Horace gets inside — too slow.**

> **We're a quarter of the way through the script and nothing has happened at all to our main characters and, more importantly, they've done nothing. What's the genre? Where's the action? Where's the story? You have to do better than this.**

What's the lesson here?

There's no more leisurely Act One anymore. We're all very busy. We're all multi-tasking. You don't have the time to present your story in infuriating dribs and drabs. You have to get right to it. Your main character doesn't have time to nap, or visit his girlfriend or boyfriend or get a haircut before the story kicks in. He or she has a mission. Neither your hero nor your reader has time to waste. Get to it. Tell your story. Show us what we paid our money to see. Don't jerk us around.

G

genre expectations

When you go to a comedy you don't expect to see a rape scene.

When you go to an action movie you don't expect to spend twenty minutes with a boy dying of AIDS.

When you go to a romance you don't expect to have to sit through a prolonged vivisection.

Part of the deal the reader/viewer has with the screenwriter has to do with these expectations. Your job as screenwriter is to fulfill the expectations of the genre — what the viewer is expecting — and also bring to it something new and fresh and your own.

You don't want to just deliver what's expected — we've seen it before. The question you should be asking yourself is: "What am I bringing to the genre that makes this a must-make script?" Set the bar high for yourself. No one's looking to hit a single, they're looking for the home run.

When you're beginning to work on your script idea, it's worth spending some time thinking about where your script is going to fit into the market place, genre-wise, and make a list of the genre expectations.

giving script notes

When you give script notes, ask the writer what kind of notes he or she is looking for.

Be constructive.

Be nice.

Be complimentary.

Be honest.

When I give notes I endeavor to keep the writer's goals in mind and create notes that come from within the idea. The context of my notes take into consideration what the screenwriter is attempting to do and what ultimately will be done with the script when it's finished.

My notes address structure, format, story and character, and anything else I see that can be improved.

My goal is to raise the level of the writing and the marketability and quality of the script.

It's not about "What *I* would do." It's about the script and making it as good as it can be.

I H

how we access your script

Here are script notes for a writer whose script was difficult to get into:

This script might be more interesting if it had more of a sense of truth than movie. The whole election thread is movie. The Nelson story is grounded in human behavior. If Nelson's personal life was as detailed as his political life, the balance of the film would be better. And most importantly, because *we access your script through the character*, there'd be a lot more for us to hook into.

Another writer I was working with was having orientation problems — guiding the reader what to pay attention to at the beginning of their script — because it was difficult to access the humanity of his script.

This was his log line:

ZING ZING SPEAKS is a true story about Laurie who learns to communicate with chimps as well as Zing Zing's story from his perspective after his starring role in the movie, ZING ZING RUNS FREE. Despite a gallant effort to release him into the wild, Zing Zing "tells" Laurie that he wants to stay with people.

My script notes:

I feel you have serious orientation problems. You're telling too much story and not telling enough of the main character's story. I think part of the issue is exemplified in the log line: Story of Laurie, that's right — and

Zing Zing's story, not right. That's two stories. You don't have time to do both stories justice so you'll want to tell Laurie's story, because she's human and we access the story through her.

Conceptually, I think you're making a mistake having any scenes with Zing Zing until Laurie's story reaches him so the reader/viewer can focus on the main character's journey.

The other big global note for you is: too many TV interviews. Reading your script is like watching television and that's not a good thing at all. Please count the number of TV interviews and lose most if not all of them. People reporting on the action rather than us experiencing it is distancing.

Whatever exposition you do need, and you surely don't need all you have, write it in other ways. I do think the story you do have to tell — what's left — is unique and interesting and worth telling.

I'd like to see you do a new scene list. I think the script starts with — take a deep breath — page 22.

Keep writing and keep thinking about writing.
Tom.

Telling your story through the main character is one of the keys of screenwriting for me.

One way to accomplish this is when you are doing your prep work before writing, try writing your scene list with the main character's name starting off every scene.

■ EXERCISE 12 — THE LAST WORD ON CREATING A MAIN CHARACTER SCENE LIST.

Take your existing script and create a quick scene list and color code every scene with your main character in it. Make sure he or she is in most of the scenes. (*See* BEGINNING YOUR SCREENPLAY)

how long should my scenes be?

Movies, you won't be surprised to read, are characterized by movement: story movement, image movement, location movement. It's why they're called *motion pictures*, it's what separates plays — stuck on a stage — from movies.

Your job as screenwriter is to keep your script moving. What bogs a script down are scenes that don't move, just sit in one place for long periods of time.

I evaluate the length of scenes this way:

The shorter the scene the better.

Most scenes should be one or two pages.

If it's an important scene, three or four pages.

If it's a scene that's one of the top ten scenes in movies — five pages.

If the scene is about the end of the world, or life discovered elsewhere in the universe — six pages.

Anything more than six pages, email me and I'll talk you down.

One of my writers didn't get the rhythm of movies. Didn't visualize her movie, didn't understand how films are made, cut together from little scenes, about moving pictures. Her script was made up of very, very, very, very talky, long scenes — fifteen pages long. Ten pages long. Interminable.

Two people sitting at a table talking for ten pages — a tenth of her whole movie — is not good movie. Not good script. (Yes,

My Dinner With André had André Gregory and Wallace Shawn sitting and talking for the length of the movie but that's the low budget, barely successful, single exception to the rule.)

I have one student now who, after my note that **the whole movie seemed to take place in two hotel rooms and felt claustrophobic,** explained that he was going to direct the film himself on a limited budget.

Made sense to me to shoot it in two hotel rooms. So I adjusted my head and gave notes with that in mind.

I was looking through the script for *The Descendants* by Alexander Payne and Nat Faxon & Jim Rash, based on a novel by Kaui Hart Hemmings, and I noticed that almost every rule I talk about in this book is broken, particularly about internal processes and We see and We hear.

The fact that Alexander Payne was involved in the script was probably a factor in why the formatting could be whatever it wanted to be.

I think the bottom line is: every rule, depending on the specific situation, can be broken without being thrown into screenwriter's jail (which entails watching every Kris Kristofferson movie ever made). The idea is *you write whatever best communicates what you need to communicate and to hell with the rules.*

how long should my script be?

Some notes I've written to writers:

Your script is too long.

And:

You should cut twenty pages.

And:

Too long.

And:

Too long!!

When I was young and stupid I'd write 145-page rough drafts. Then, I had the unenviable task of developing the script further at the same time cutting 45 pages. How inefficient a process is that?

Now, I try to write an 85-page rough draft. That's right, just 85 pages. Then, over the process of rewriting, I have 20 pages of gold to add where I need to.

I try to shoot for a script coming in around 106 pages.

Scripts that run over a 115 pages are tough sledding.

Anything over 130 pages is abusive.

What I wrote to a writer:

Hi Lonnie -

Good idea for a movie. Lots of work to do. At 140 pages you're very long. Very, very long. Your pages

are four lines longer than my program, which is industry standard.

Multiply that by 140 pages and you could add maybe another ten pages. So at 150 you're nearly 40 pages too long. Way, way, way too long. One in every three pages has to be eliminated. See the issue?

I want you to picture the life of Script Readers in Hollywood. They work for the studio and producers and their job is to read and report on your script. They're the industry's first line of defense. The reader takes home a pile of, let's say, fifteen scripts to whip through over the weekend. They pour a glass of wine and settle in the backyard next to the small pool for an afternoon of script assassination. They heft your script. More than likely they're a little put off the by the weight. They know precisely what 105 pages feels like. They flip to the end of your script. FADE OUT is on page 137. They sag. 137 pages?!? Strike one. This better be good.

They take a sip of wine and turn to the first page and see dense, oh so dense scene description. They GROAN. You want them to enjoy the experience of reading your script so their report is positive. Now you have two strikes against you.

They leaf quickly through the pages. All the scene descriptions are dense. The dialogue blocks are oh so very long. Speechifying. Strike three. Your script is outta there. It goes to the bottom of her pile — never to be read.

Be smart, write short.

I

internal processes

A screenwriter wrote in his script:

> Rebecca wants to pull away and <u>intuitively</u> knows
> she shouldn't.

And...

> Rebecca <u>imagines</u> the worst…she can't help
> herself.

And...

> Rebecca <u>pretends</u> that she cares.

The problem with that kind of writing is it describes internal processes — intuitively knows, imagines, pretends — not able to be filmed. How would a director film "Rebecca imagines"? or "intuitively knows"? What does the camera see?

Your job is to report what's up on the screen. What we see. Forget writing about internal processes. Movies are about behavior and movement. Describe what you see and hear, not what's happening inside your character's head.

Another writer wrote:

> She tries to <u>remember</u> a time when her mother
> wasn't so critical, but can't.

And filming a person trying to remember?

How about this:

> When someone gets this far down, one of two
> things happens. He gives up completely. Or he
> gets angry.

Or...

> Without warning he becomes the killer in his
> mind.

Tough to film.

How does a director shoot:

> Viking <u>understands</u> he'll never leave her...?

■ EXERCISE 13 — THE LAST WORD ON INTERNAL PROCESSES.

Check the script you're writing, or the last draft of your latest script and do a search for all the words underlined above. Make sure you're not writing internal processes. (*Please see* NOVELISTIC WRITING)

it's a process

Screenwriters want to be potato farmers when they write pages and they're not what they want them to be.

Screenwriters yearn to be beekeepers when people don't get what they write.

Screenwriters go kayaking when they get bored writing and rewriting the same pages over and over again.

Screenwriters eat too much ice cream when they write and write and it's still not right.

Screenwriters age before their time when they write and write and the pages are lousy.

What I've told hundreds of writers and will tell hundreds more is that SCREENWRITING IS A PROCESS. Just keep writing and eventually it's all going to start to come together.

You don't have a lot of words to communicate what you need to communicate — be precise.

I've written novels where you have tons and tons of pages and tons of words to tell your story. You're not limited by pages, or time, or being able to write only what's on the screen, you can write your brains out.

But when you're writing a screenplay, you don't have that luxury. You have to be disciplined, selective and ruthless. You only have time for what is necessary. It takes me pass after pass to achieve the kind of sleek script needed to send out. (*Please see* WEIGHTING YOUR WRITING)

I tell writers to take chances, to experiment, because they will come back to these pages time and time again because, as I've said — yes, that's right — SCREENWRITING IS A PROCESS.

it's not about
your writing

Below is a sample from a writer's script. The writing was pretty much all like this:

```
Now a cell camera. SNAP. SNAP. The Person. The
sign. Got it. Now an email. JRUBY.NSA.COM Send
it. Done. A distant bell tolls.
```

It was exhausting to read.

This is a global note for your script: Your writing is calling attention to your writing, rather than the story you're telling. It's creative, it's different, and I have no idea what your story is. It's all smoke and mirrors of language taking away from your story rather than enhancing it. They are words, not images. I have to stop the flow of reading your script to figure out what the hell it means.

```
Looks like she (referring to a girl) was ridden
hard and put away wet.
```

Same thing. One of the issues of fancy shmancy writing is that it doesn't appear on the screen and it makes the script pale in comparison.

```
Trevor kicks himself.
```

What do we see on the screen? Surely not Trevor kicking himself. Your job is to report what we see and hear on the screen.

It's not about words — it's about seeing, reporting what we see.

L

less is more

On the brink, Mother doesn't manage to object —
there's an old man's voice coming from outside:

```
            OLD MAN
    Mrs. Lorimar! I say Mrs. Lorimar, are
    you in there? Are you in there?
```

Thirty-two words. A little flabby for my tastes.

It should read:

```
Mother doesn't object.

            OLD MAN'S VOICE
         (from outside)
    Mrs. Lorimar?
```

Ten words. Less than a third. And what have we lost?
Nothing.

What "Less is more" means to a screenwriter is the need to
be concise — the ability to communicate more of what you want
to as simply and elegantly as you can. To be able to say what
you need to say, sell the important parts, minimize the lesser
parts, disclose the information in dramatic ways — you're moving toward having a good screenplay.

While I'm thinking about it: **What is a good screenplay?**
Is it one that sells? That's good, for sure.
Is it one that's well-written? That's good, too.

How about one that gets you work, a calling card script? Very good.

What about one that doesn't get you work, is well-written — or at least the best you can do — is that one good? You bet it is.

Every time you write, every single time you write, you get better. Some part of your ability to write a screenplay improves every time you exercise it.

It's mathematical when it comes to writing your screenplay: the more you write on it the better it gets. The more you write, the better writer you become. Keep writing. Keep showing up every day. That's what it takes.

It brings up the question: What if after twenty years of writing screenplays, you haven't sold a screenplay? Nothing. Some people like them. Maybe an Honorable Mention in a screenplay contest. But, after twenty years, no real success. Has that time been wasted?

To me, twenty years of writing is a gift you've been given of being able to spend your journey creating stories and characters and being totally engaged and challenged and working and learning and having fun and producing something that wasn't there before. Not so terrible.

let your actors act

Alexandra is stunned.

                    ALEXANDRA
          I don't know if I should be scared
          out of my mind or amazed.

I'd cut this dialogue. Let the actress look stunned. She doesn't need to voice it.

          Looking staggeringly beautiful, Lindsay walks
          into the living room. Harold smiles.

                    HAROLD
          You look lovely.

The dialogue is unneeded. An Executive Producer of a series I worked on, Leon Tokatyan, used to call that kind of writing "Eggs on eggs," too much of a good thing, redundant to the extreme. How about Harold looks adoringly at Lindsay instead of dialogue?

The actor should be able to communicate "You look lovely" without words. Actors are always looking for the "juice" in a scene. Cutting the dialogue and having the actor act makes for a better film and happier actors.

You should try thinking about what you write as not words on a page but as reality, as scenes, as people behaving together in the environment.

Watch some silent movies. They communicate so much story, emotion, character. No words other than the occasional title.

log lines

(Please see BEGINNING YOUR SCREENPLAY *for how to create a log line)*

A student wrote:

"Please give me some insight into log lines."

Okay.

"Are these studio executives basically reading the log line and tossing it if it doesn't fit a '13-year-old boy' audience?"

Some of them might be. However, I'm not sure studio executives are so hooked into log lines. It's more a writer's tool, than a marketing tool.

"If my script is a mystery, should I give away the ending in my log line?"

Yes. You're looking to sell your script. Tell the story the most satisfying way you can in your log line so that you give your idea every chance.

"Do I basically just enhance the log line with a couple sentences for a pitch?"

You want to think in terms of beginning, middle and end, memorable scenes as well as why it's news.

"Are there tricks to grab their attention?"

The trick is having a good story to pitch.

The log line is a vital writer's tools. It allows you to help clarify exactly what you're writing about.

main characters

(*Please see* CHARACTER)

One of the writers in my Master Class was writing a script with an absent main character.

> **Paula's barely in this script. She's constantly being lied to by both Hiram and Stella and never gets it — for basically the whole movie while we know exactly what's going on. Makes us think she's an idiot, which is not a good thing. That, coupled with the fact that she doesn't change much, is very problematic. I'd like you to re-think this so that this script is about Paula and we access this script through her character.**

TELLING THE STORY THROUGH THE MAIN CHARACTER

Another writer I was working with was writing a civil war drama. It was pretty good until I realized I wasn't rooting for anyone, or for that matter following any particular character, which worked for a while, but then felt less than.

> **About this point, I'm definitely feeling the lack of someone I can identify with, someone to root for, someone to hate, characters I can hook into. You're telling a story without main characters we can enter the story through.**

A note to another writer:

> **I'm feeling the script is too open. I'm seeing the whole story from a universal perspective. I, as the reader/**

viewer know everything, rather than playing along with the main character. I'd like to see you take a third of your script and re-scene list it so that Rulanda is in the middle of your story — that it's really Rulanda's story. Before you start this adjustment, reconfigure your log line so that it's Rulanda's story as well. After you've rewritten a third of it — evaluate how it's working to see if you want to proceed on with the rest.

And another:

Norman, your main character, has to be more front and center and more proactive. More heroic. More interesting. More obsessed. Stronger. More dominant. He should drive this script — and doesn't. Dig deeper.

And a third:

The whole opening is questionable to me because it focuses on Blaine, a character who never returns except for the mention of his name later. The first scene has no dialogue for our hero Andre. Not sure that's how to orient the piece.

That brings up a big issue for me: Do we really want to spend 90 minutes with a loser who remains a loser — with no variation and no character movement until the very end? It's not that he tries to change and fails. He just mopes through the movie not doing anything. Is that enough to hold us, or do you need to give us more attempts, stabs at proactivity, standing up for himself and failing?

metaphors and similes

One of my screenwriters wrote:

```
INT. CHEESY BAR — NIGHT
Soaked by Pancho's drink, Red runs at him like a
rhinoceros in heat.
```

Really? The problem with that or "Sprints like a gazelle" **or** "Waddles like a platypus" **or any simile or metaphor is that it places an image in the reader's mind that doesn't appear in the movie. Don't do it.**

And another writer's work:

```
The elevator opens and it seems like everyone
inside jumps off into the lobby as if the Queen
of England is inside.
```

So now I'm visualizing the Queen of England.

```
Everything seems to slow down.
```

Are you saying it's slow motion?

A variation from another writer:

```
The rain looked like melted teardrops on the
window.
```

Melted teardrops — really? No, not really. Makes me come out of your screenplay to think about your writing. Nice imagery. Inappropriate for your script. Some more images that don't belong in your screenplay:

Possum-like.
Like a nosy neighbor.
Like an out of control basketball.
Like a happy puppy dog.

montages

I had a writer who was montage crazy. It seemed every ten pages or so there'd be a major montage: a boring, non-selling, throw-away list of scenes. Get a sense how I feel about this?

I emailed the writer:

Montages work much better in film than in scripts. In films, there's music and the editor and director can put together a well-designed, cut-to-the-music sequence that's cinematic and entertaining. The screenwriter has none of those tools to work with — just words.

Montages don't work as well in screenplays because they break the normal script format and become a list — no music, no beautiful imagery and transitions — just a flat, usually numbered, list of action with no normal slug lines. This effectively takes the reader out of the script rather than keeps them in. Montages are usually little more than a dry list of scenes. *I think it's more effective to write out the scenes and don't break form*. Leave the montages to the filmmakers.

I wrote to a writer who felt she needed to montage the main character's childhood as a way for her to introduce her.

There's something obvious and clichéd about this montage of important moments in Elinor's past. You're telling a story and we're into it, then suddenly the hand of the writer shows itself and presents a list of scenes — breaking format and jarring the reader — saying

here are the important moments of the main character's childhood. Who asked?

I think that kind of format-busting, unneeded distraction is counterproductive at best and suicidal at worst. Well, maybe not suicidal, but pretty darn bad.

Another writer was writing a really good caper movie. When he got to the heist, suddenly he broke form and listed the action of the caper in a flat and boring way.

I wrote:

Isn't the fun of heist movies to see how the intricate plan is carried out in all its minute techno-details? The montage distances us from the heart of this script. We feel we're not seeing the whole deal. The clever details of the heist are what will make this script memorable.

morris the explainer

One of my favorite students was writing a detective thriller with a private eye as the main character. In the end scene, another character, the femme fatale, takes center stage and explains to us what happened in the movie. I told the screenwriter that the wrong character was playing Morris. It really should be the private eye who explains the case and the movie is the story of his procedural investigation and how he attained the information.

And to another writer:

You have Leonardo explaining too much. By now in the script, something comes up and we all turn to Leonardo to explain and he does. Too easy. Too convenient. Work harder. Then, later, two new characters — mother and father — come in and explain the rest if the movie to us. This is not right either.

When I was a kid, one of the staples on late-night television was those fabulously weird, probably racist Charlie Chan movies. They were characterized by the closing scene where Charlie, that wonderfully stereotypical Chinese Private Eye, would gather all the suspects in the living room of the mansion of the dead man and step by step explain who did what to who and at the last moment, right before he's going to reveal the murderer's name, the lights flash off and there are two shots in the darkness. When the candles are finally lit by the Butler, Lady Montgomery is dead on the floor and her diamond necklace is gone.

After the police arrive, the ever-inscrutable Charlie Chan weaves a hypnotic tale of wrong-doing and skullduggery for the befuddled Police Captain, then reveals the murderer as none other than Reginald Westbrook, the ne'er-do-well playboy polo star, who pulls a gun but is overpowered by Grant, the handsome heir to the Montgomery fortune.

There are better ways to do it than Charlie Chan or Morris the Explainer. There are more interesting ways to distribute the information as we go so we feed the reader/viewer clues — engaging them — making the journey infinitely more pleasurable.

movie recommendations

A totally subjective list of films I recommend:

Annie Hall — Woody Allen at his best.

Truly, Madly, Deeply — Anthony Minghella's warm-hearted love story.

The Godfather and *The Godfather Part 2* — Coppola's masterpieces.

Manhattan — More great Woody Allen.

The Deer Hunter — Michael Cimino's quintessential American saga.

La Dolce Vita — One of Fellini's best.

Death In Venice — Visconti's fantastic mood piece.

2001: A Space Odyssey — Kubrick. The most perfect movie ever made.

Citizen Kane — Orson Welles. The second most perfect movie ever made.

Double Indemnity — Billy Wilder. Raymond Chandler. Great film noir.

The Truman Show — Andrew Niccol, writer. One of my recent favorites.

Close Encounters Of The Third Kind — Spielberg at his peak.

Last Tango In Paris — Bernardo Bertolucci's masterpiece. Brando.

Everything Is Illuminated — Liev Schreiber directs. Quirky and wonderful and odd.

Moonstruck — The most romantic movie ever made. Jewison, Shanley.

Hannah And Her Sisters — Yet another wonderful Woody Allen.

The Right Stuff — Philip Kaufman's soaring contemporary epic.

Sunset Boulevard — Great Hollywood movie. Wilder, Swanson, Holden.

The Social Network — I've told you how much I like this movie. Sorkin/Fincher.

Apocalypse Now — Another seminal movie from Francis Ford Coppola.

The Last Waltz — The best music video ever made, bar none. Scorsese.

A Night At The Opera — The Marx Brothers. Talk about funny.

Duck Soup — More Marx Brothers. Even funnier.

All About Eve — Joe Mankiewicz, Bette Davis. Mesmerizing.

Mr. Hulot's Holiday — The genius of Jacques Tati.

Adaptation. — Charlie Kaufman is one of the best writers around.

Day For Night — Francois Truffaut's fantastic ode to the movies.

Top Hat — Fred Astaire and Ginger Rogers at their best.

Being John Malkovich — Another Charlie Kaufman mindbender.

The Purple Rose Of Cairo — Woody Allen's valentine to the movies.

Lawrence Of Arabia — David Lean is the master.

Fanny and Alexander — Bergman's masterwork. See the 5-hour version.

Some Like It Hot — Marilyn Monroe. Billy Wilder again.

Random Harvest — With one of the greatest moments in the history of movies. And you'll have to see it to find out what it is.

my script feels familiar, what do i do?

One of my online students wrote me an urgent email.

"My script feels familiar, what do I do?"

She was desperate. It was a realization she came to reading the first thirty pages before she sent them to me. She was very down about it. I read the pages.

You're right. These pages do feel too familiar. Good of you to be able to recognize that. Your opening scene is way too much like the scene in the wonderful, Oscar-winning movie *Annie Hall* — written by Woody Allen and Marshall Brickman — when Woody visits Diane Keaton's majorly WASP-ish family. A classic. We all know it. Yours reads too much like it.

And to another writer, I wrote:

Good scene, but it's too much like the transformation scene in *Pretty Woman*. You're going to have to change it.

And to the same writer:

This scene feels like I've seen it a hundred times before. The first scene that comes up in your mind isn't always the best. Work harder. It feels that your default position as a writer is to write what you've already seen. You need to go through your script and spin those scenes so they feel fresh and new.

One of the difficulties in screenwriting is that so many script and story ideas feel familiar. It's hard to think you're doing anything original. What do you do? *You have to spin your idea.*

Born Yesterday, from a great Garson Kanin play and Alan Mannheimer script, is about industrialist Paul Douglas hiring egghead William Holden to educate and polish his diamond-in-the-rough girlfriend wonderfully played by the amazing Judy Holliday.

I wanted to write a *Born Yesterday*–adjacent movie, one that uses the strength of the idea but doesn't feel like the same movie at all.

So, I spun the idea: A girl hires a male shrink to polish up her pig-like boyfriend, a professional athlete. It's different enough not to be an instant reminder of *Born Yesterday*. But I had a lot more spinning to do: changing all the personal and professional details of the original movie, all the character traits, locations, incidents. When I finished the script, and sent it out, only one reader mentioned *Born Yesterday*, and not in a negative way. The script ultimately got optioned and, at one point, I sold the short film rights and a film was made. It was called *Rita, Pigboy and Me*.

A way to attack spinning an idea: isolate your attraction to the original idea. What is it about the movie, on the most basic level, that intrigues you? Then change everything else.

The last reaction you want to your script is "Feels like So and So movie."

■ EXERCISE 14 – THE LAST WORD ON SPINNING A FAMILIAR MOVIE IDEA.

Take a popular movie, or one of your favorites, and spin the idea. See how much you can change it without losing its appeal.

I N

names

Karl and Carla. Donna and Deena. Roland and Ronald. Tom and Tim.

The idea about the way you name your characters is to not confuse people who are reading your script fast, but to make their job easier by differentiating between the names as much as possible.

I had one writer whose characters inexplicably all had names which began with B's: Ben, Brad, Brian, Bella, Babs, Bea. It was damn near impossible to read the script.

Then, there are the funny names in scripts: Jesus Dingleberry. Fred Flapass. Molly Mammaries.

I don't think so.

It's way too easy and way too stupid to name characters this way. Since many full names never are spoken aloud in scripts, the inclusion of knee-slappin' names is distracting at best and destructive at worst. It's a tonal issue. If you have a character named Carla Crotch, what do you expect the reader to feel or think?

I file it under the heading of Cheesy.

narrative pull

Narrative pull is the energy of your script that makes the reader turn the page, pulling them through the screenplay. It's what moves the script forward.

A big note to an online writer:
The largest note I have is that I feel the need for an overriding narrative thread — something we know about her at the beginning that pays off at the end, and that you service a few times during the body of the story. It will help pull us through the script.

I wrote to another writer:
The house number — an example of what I mean, but not what I really mean — for the narrative pull in this story is: Francois always wanted to have New Year's Eve in Paris and in the end you pull back to reveal it's New Year's Eve at the top of the Eiffel Tower. Of course, you service that narrative thread throughout the script.

And to another screenwriter:
The overall narrative need/dream/want could be tied to the trunk of finery she embraces and smells at one point, or it could be that she's all over Lance at the beginning that she needs a real home — you know, white picket fence, garden — not this patch of hell in the middle of the desert. At the end we realize she's finally made the desert her home. Whatever you choose, this narrative line has to be serviced regularly and build to a climax.

Another writer kept interrupting the narrative pull with mind flashes, which, like backstory and flashbacks, don't work for me.

> **Now on page 45 there's yet another short blast of Tommy's mind in italics. This doesn't work at all. By continually — this is now the third time — breaking into the narrative pull of this movie you're not giving the story any chance to gather momentum. Trust your story and let it work. You're splintering the storytelling and I'm not sure why. It doesn't get you anything.**

An online consultation was writing a script that kept introducing characters. Nothing resonated, nothing evolved, there was no narrative pull.

> **Who are all these people and what are they doing? Scenes happen with no action. It's not enough to just introduce character after character. They have to move the story forward. We're 16 pages in and I'm unable to put the scenes into any coherent story. Time to take another look.**

This writer was jumping back and forth between the past and the present and it didn't allow the story to have any narrative pull.

> **The big question you have to ask yourself is: Does the structural conceit you've imposed on the story work? Does it enhance the story or distract from it? Does it make for a better or easier or more pleasurable reading/viewing experience? The answer for me is clearly "No."**
>
> *The structural conceit doesn't allow for continued emotional/character investment in terms of the reader/ viewer.*
>
> **Just as a story gets going, the script cuts away and starts another unrelated story. It would be one thing if the stories coalesced into a single story at the end**

and the resonances and evolution of the different stories intertwined — but they don't. They don't even attempt to.

The story opens focusing on Oliver, a character we never see again, which can't be a good thing, the murder of a character we don't care about, then we meet George, who is a terrific character but with only the slightest connection to the first story — a connection which ceases immediately. Not only do the characters introduced in the first story not appear in the second story, it suddenly becomes a Mel Brooks musical, which after the realistic/violent first section is disorienting at best. Then after the fun of the musical numbers, it turns into bloody mayhem and then — a vampire movie.

What is it you want me to think or feel other than get me out of here? What am I supposed to invest in? Who am I supposed to invest in? If the idea is to surprise the reader/viewer and throw them off, disorient them, well, then maybe it accomplishes what it sets out to do. I'm just not sure that's what you want to do with the reader/viewer. I think you want to engage the reader/viewer and not push them away.

For me, when you have all these stories, they should relate, characters should run through from one story to another, they should intertwine and evolve and coalesce into one story. (See Robert Altman's wonderful multiple-story film *Nashville*)

In the best of all possible worlds the stories would resonate with each other, feed and evolve together. What's missing for me, and this is really important, is that there's no NARRATIVE PULL. There's no arcing, evolving reason to care, to read on.

Another screenwriter was writing a script about Genghis Khan. I gave him notes telling him the story was way too slow in starting and what he was having happen on page twenty-seven should actually be happening on pages seven to ten. My notes were about not writing set-up and waiting until the story met up with the information organically or exposition — most of which is absolutely unneeded for us to understand the characters because we can understand who characters are by their behavior.

He responded by explaining very carefully why he wrote everything he wrote. *"Page 1 sets the environment. Pages 2–4 set the tone. Page 5–6 set up the theme."*

I responded:

I've read a lot of scripts. I pretty much get what you're doing. Just because there's a reasoned rationale to what you're doing doesn't it make it good script.

He went on:

"Genghis Khan's existence is one of history's most investigated stories, so the historical, the literal and the mythical aspects of the story are what I wanted to show in these pages."

Yes, I know. That's evident. The problem is: it's not the story. You should be telling the story from the get-go and all the historical, literal and mythical aspects of Genghis Khan should come into the story when the story naturally meets them. That's different than what you're doing.

The result of doing that would mean you would get to the story you really want to write — the log line — right away. That's a more contemporary structure than all this very, very slow set-up.

FOLLOW-UP: The writer ignored my desperate pleas for screenwriting sanity and now happily works as a history teacher in Coral Gables, Florida. He continues writing unproduced historical scripts at night. They're all very heavy with exposition. He's very happy.

non-linear storytelling

A screenwriter was working on the early stage of his idea and was searching for the way to write it. He wrote.

"Would it help if the story went in a non-linear style where Sam was introduced in the beginning of the script?"

Good question. Nice to see you exploring your options. In my opinion, a non-linear structure further distances the reader/viewer from the material, making it harder for them to get it. For me, non-linear increases your problems. There's no forward momentum, no way I can put together the story in any linear way. I'm forced to put together what feels like random scenes. Why are you making it so hard? And what do you gain by doing it this way? It seems to be more about style than substance. (*See* SPLINTERING TIME)

novelistic writing

Novelistic writing is writing that employs literary, unable-to-be-filmed description, like the writing in novels, that isn't appropriate for a screenplay.

> On the tip of his shoes, a little bit of dried dirt hints that he is not the "teach-because-can't-do" type of professor. He teaches what he knows, he teaches what he's personally researched and explored.

Not in the movie — too novelistic.

> The action moves to the destroyed holiday village.

You have to write this as script not as a "chapter heading."

> He dreams to find the lizard he found out about from the secret archives of FBI.

Dreams? That's an internal process that's impossible to film. Too novelistic. Rewrite please. (*See* INTERNAL PROCESSES)

> His life's purpose as a ship's captain is now very much in jeopardy.

Lines like the above are too novelistic and unable to be filmed.

> They are thought of as invaders or even conquerors.
> With their weapons in hand, they surely don't seem to offer peace.

If I were the director, I'd be flummoxed trying to film this. Too novelistic.

```
Trying to capture his soul that has already
left, he settles in his mind for a record of the
corpse.
```
Way, way too novelistic.

What's the lesson here?

You have to solve the storytelling with elements that will appear in the film. If you want to know the truth: I think novelistic writing is cheating because the writer has used writing that doesn't appear on the screen to solve story problems.

10

on-the-nose writing

Early on in his script, the screenwriter wrote this scene:

```
The Priest hands Sam a crucifix. Sam throws it
against the wall.

               SAM
     You can live with misperceptions if
     you want, Father, but if God existed,
     he wouldn't have allowed a Nun to
     hurt my little sister, or some
     freakin' creep to stab my brother.

Sam hands the crucifix back to the Priest.

               SAM (CONT'D)
     My belief died when Lacy took her
     own life. Where was your God then?
```

My script note:

This feels so on-the-nose, so expositiony, telling us exactly what the character is thinking — in detail. Think about holding off the specific information and make the scene about his hatred of the church, throwing the information above into subtext, or what's unspoken behind the scenes. Listen to people speak. They rarely say exactly what they mean.

Every character shouldn't have to articulate their feelings on screen. Really, none should. Let us find out about the specifics later. Arc the information.

I'd like to see you take another pass on the dialogue to see if you can write it so they don't say precisely what they mean. Imply more so the reader/viewer isn't given exactly what is going on, but given a little less and has to work a little harder.

Another screenwriter wrote:

```
Olivia starts up the stairs. Lawrence grabs her
leg to restrain her.

                    LAWRENCE
         Are you sure you want to risk Your
         life? You're so young.
```

My note:

Lawrence is saying exactly what he's thinking. It's a literary rather than a behavioral response to the situation. We know that's what Lawrence is thinking because we're probably thinking the same thing, but you don't need to have the character say it. Something like this might be better.

```
                    LAWRENCE
         My God, don't!
```

Another writer:

```
                    HORACE
         Pictures, lovely as they are, sure
         are cruel reminders of what we no
         longer touch, or smell. If only we
         could bring him back.
```

This maudlin dialogue is too on-the-nose for my tastes. This character is saying exactly what he means (and I won't speak to his poetic nature which feels like something out of the 18th Century). Real people don't talk so directly or articulately. They beat around the bush, obfuscate, take the long way around, don't speak in complete sentences. (*Please see* APPROPRIATE LANGUAGE)

open stories
versus closed stories

Deciding how to tell your story — the point of view of your script — is one of the most important choices you make as a screenwriter.

Here are some notes I've written to different writers:

You've written this piece as an open script — watching all facets of the story — protagonist, antagonist, everything. I'd like to see you re-evaluate that choice and consider closing the script — just showing the protagonist's story. I think with us going along on the main character's journey, it's going to be a much more exciting script.

And to another writer:

Because you've written this as an open story — we know everything there is to know. I think it really dilutes the mystery.

And another:

Right now it's an open script. We know everything that's happening. Sheila doesn't know. Shouldn't we be playing along with her?

And another.

I think the story should be more personal. Take your scene list and close it down — so we don't see her mother's side of the story and see what happens. I think it will focus your script and make it much more dramatic.

And, finally:

**Good job. I think the script is very well written —
extremely well written in fact and that's something I
don't get to say often enough. The issue in your script
is not the craft of writing, but what you're writing. I
think you need to shore up a lot of the storytelling and
seriously consider closing the story down so that we
see it more from Alana's point of view. You reveal too
much story to the reader/viewer, vitiating the suspense
and mystery. My suggestion is to create a closed scene
list presenting only Alana's point of view and see how it
reads to you.**

Open stories versus closed is all about the information you
supply to the reader. My personal bias is to tell the story through
the main character only — a closed story — because it makes
the read more interesting and interactive for the reader.

overhearing

Daniela overhears the conversation between Anne
and Mickey and breaks into tears.

**I'm not a big fan of overhearing. It's such an easy, conve-
nient way for a character to learn something. I'd like
you to consider changing it so there's a scene between
Anne and Mickey where they argue, and Mickey is really
angry so he tells Daniela he's going away to the army.**

Overhearing is a maddeningly common device: the main
character overhears major story moments that change the story
and allows him or her to accomplish their mission. I've never
overheard a major moment in my life. How about you?

P

pace

I finished reading a writer's script and I was exhausted. It was a tough read. Dense, slow, and to make it worse: long. Way long.

My biggest note for you is this script is too long. It's 135 pages and it should be 105. It should read fast and breezy and it doesn't. It's tedious at best. How many scenes in bars, restaurants, liquor stores and mini-markets do you have of him drinking beer? What happened to all his meetings?

Next draft — save this one — you should go through and cut the hell out of it. In this draft, we're 35 minutes — a minute a page — in and haven't gotten to the 'A' story yet. Not good.

That writer's not alone:

I'm on page 26 and your story is moving slowly, very slowly. From the time they decide to go to the fair it's taken four pages. You have to have your story move faster. Cut right to the fair. Get into it. Cut to the heart of the scene.

It's a very common issue:

And now the convention begins — nine pages since it was originally brought up! What important happened in those nine pages? Nothing. Why couldn't you cut right to the opening of the convention? You've got to pick up the pace of these pages.

Sometimes, I'm not happy to admit, I lose patience with a writer:

Your script is slow and painfully linear. Every 'I' is dotted. Every 'T' is crossed. For a disaster-type action script, there's no urgency, no energy. It's way too lackadaisical in terms of audience expectations of the genre. (*See* GENRE EXPECTATIONS) **Your hero has time to sleep with some bimbo? You're going to have to crank up the pace or your pages are going to end up in the dumpster.**

I apologized to this writer and helped him move his script in the right direction.

This writer paid no attention to pace and rhythm:

The storytelling in your script is oddly paced. The story evolves slowly — the doctor's physical is fifteen pages long when it could accomplish the same thing in three pages. Before that, there's pages and pages of set-up. The movie feels like it's in real time. You should think about a more comedic pacing.

Another student wrote:

"Hey Tom, just wanted to bounce something off you that I'm second guessing. Should I be concerned about all the location jumping? New York to Philly to Denver and finally back to New York. I like it busy, but not sure if it's a little much."

I like it. It moves. I think it helps and is good.

A MOVIE RECOMMENDATION

I can't help but take advantage of this forum to recommend a wonderful, underappreciated movie I revisited recently. *Everything Is Illuminated*, adapted and directed by Liev Schreiber. The pace is positively meditative. I recommend that you see this movie. It's a fabulously quirky and interesting change of pace. With an amazing soundtrack. An original.

(parentheses)

```
        FREDRIC
(gets back a little in order
to have a better look, but
still embraces Katya)

        MARTIN
(points out the Police sign)
```

This material should not be in parentheses. It is scene description. *Parentheses are solely for explaining dialogue.*

```
        AVA
(using her va-va voom
voluptuous body parts to
their best advantage)
```

The parentheses you're using as asides to the reader — which won't appear in the film — are a little needy for my tastes. There's a lot of "love me," self-conscious writing in here that calls attention to the writing and the writer rather than the story and the movie. (*Please see* IT'S NOT ABOUT YOUR WRITING)

```
Rita (17), a sow of a girl, eats a double
cheeseburger.
```

Why is the age in parentheses? A lot of people are doing that and I don't get it. It's as if the age of character is not really part of the script or is an aside. Makes no sense to me.

It should read:

Rita, 17, a sow of a girl, eats pepperoni pizza.

                    TOM
                 (angrily)
          Stop using parentheses for scene
          description.

perfectionism

A writer I was working with had finished her first time through and started asking me where she thought I should send her script.

> **This script is not to ready to send out. There are format issues, misspellings, missing words, and, most important — unrealized scenes with unpolished dialogue. You're only part way there. You're not finished. Go back to work. Your script has to be perfect before you send it out.**

Please don't make the mistake too many inexperienced screenwriters make and send out your script before it's finished — and by finished I mean you make every scene perfect. Every line perfect. Every word the perfect word.

After the long, lonely process of writing a script, people send out scripts early to get praise. Please don't do that. Wait until it's absolutely perfect. You only get one fresh read per reader. Don't waste it.

pitching

Pitching isn't writing. It's performance, organization, and clean clothes.

Usually, but not always, you pitch a project before you write it. If that's the case you really have to do your homework so you give the pitchee enough for them to make a decision and for you to be able to answer their questions when you're finished pitching.

I've pitched a lot. Here's what I do.

To prepare a pitch for a project I haven't written yet: I create character biographies so I know who the main character is and I can tell the story through him or her.

I create a scene list using the three-act structure. I've found this is more comfortable/familiar for communicating to the pitchee. If I sell the piece, I abandon the three-act structure for Rising Action — but don't tell anyone.

In that three-act structure I've prepared for pitching, I isolate a beginning, middle, and end for the three-acts: nine scenes. I then tell that story through the main character. That's the core of my pitch.

I also prepare a separate version of what I'm pitching that describes the main character's journey as well as who the antagonist is and what they do to put the hero in jeopardy.

Then, with preparatory work done, I script my pitch. I get it perfect, so it presents everything I want the pitch to accomplish — then, I memorize it.

I can't tell you how many pitches my dogs have heard — and they're a tough audience.

Once I've perfected my pitch, I take my pitch script and put PITCH NOTES on the top and bring a copy to the meeting as a "leave behind."

I try to keep my pitch down to six minutes. The executives you pitch in Hollywood, as a rule, have attention spans of a maggot, so you have to get in and get out and present the goods as dramatically and as memorably as possible.

I whip myself into a frenzy of excitement, coffee, and courage, and go for it. Once in the office of the person or persons I'm pitching, I try and be cooled out but it's tough. I do my best to make small talk, but usually I find that difficult because I know they want me out of there as soon as possible and the schmoozing I'm supposed to be doing isn't on my agenda. I'll try and remark about something in their office: "Nice art," or "Oh, you're a Lakers fan," or some such thing, then usually a couple of minutes after I've sat down — don't sit on the couch, too low. Try and sit on the chair — I can't help myself and say, "Let's talk about what I'm here to pitch you." Not the best approach. I advise following the lead of the person you're pitching.

Then, with my pitch notes in my lap in case I get lost, I pitch. You usually can tell if the person you're pitching to is interested. Too many times I've had executive's eyes glaze over and tell me to continue as they make a phone call to their Jaguar or Mercedes dealer.

Most of the time, everyone loves the pitch. Only nice things to say. Makes you feel good. Rarely do you get a "Yes" or "No" in the room. "Yes" has only happened twice. I found it so hard to believe I had to have the Exec repeat what she said.

I finish pitching, leave behind my Pitch Notes and exit. The reason I leave them behind is that if the pitchee wants to pitch his or her boss, they'll have notes to pitch from versus their spotty memory.

BREAKING NEWS!

While writing this book, I got a call from an L.A. production company, producers of two recent hits. A friend had introduced me and I sent them my latest script *Hollywood Capone*. They called for a meeting, which was yesterday. I was prepared to talk about *Capone*, but also brought in another script of mine *My Totally Mutant Life in the 4th Dimension*, and was also prepared to pitch a third — an unwritten script — a sports story — as their last big hit was a sports story. I wanted to make the most of this chance.

I was ushered into their very large Century City offices and nervously awaited my meeting. Within a respectful amount of time two Creative Executives — that's what it said on their cards — came in. Together, their age didn't add up to mine, but I pressed on. They talked about the business, moguls, gangsters, shmoozy stuff until I got antsy. Figuring they weren't interested in *Capone* or they would have indicated so, I said I wanted to talk about the script in the envelope I had brought which was on the conference table in front of me.

They were a little surprised at my taking over the meeting, but they were cool.

I pitched them *Totally Mutant Life*. They said they'd read it. I didn't sense any great interest. Polite interest, at best. Then I pitched them the sports story. Their eyes glazed over. Oh, well.

They asked if I had any thrillers.

Now, bear in mind, I've written over fifty original screenplays — so I reached back into the dark recesses of my caffeine-soaked brain and remembered *Christopher* — the story of a therapist who is treating a psychopath who claims responsibility for a series of grisly murders. Oh, by the way, the psychopath is 12 years old.

That's my short-hand pitch — what do you think?
They loved it. And as I type this they are reading it.

TEN DAYS LATER
I've heard nothing. No news is no news.

ANOTHER WEEK GOES BY
Still silence. I would have hoped they'd read it right away and called. Hmmmmm.

TWO MORE WEEKS GOES BY
Maybe they've read it and are figuring out how much money to offer me for the option.

A MONTH MORE PASSES
Still no word. I think I'll email the guy and ask if he read it. What do I have to lose?

THREE WEEKS LATER
I didn't email them. If they wanted to be in bed with me they would have called. I hate this business.

ANOTHER MONTH GOES BY
I've heard nothing. So, I take my .357 Magnum and hide in the bushes outside their offices, then think better of it and go home. That was a close one. (See the movie *The Player*)

FINAL UPDATE — ANOTHER MONTH HAS GONE BY
Silence. I never heard anything. What have I learned? Silence is the new "No."

play the joke

I had a writer in a couple of my classes who had a good idea for a movie — the main character would put on his grandfather's hat and would be transported back in time. He initially wanted to play it twice in the movie. I urged him — some would say browbeat — to use the gag at least half a dozen times. He did. The script was good and ultimately got made. I wish I could take total credit, but I can't. He did a great job with the script. And those six scenes played great.

I wrote to another writer:

You have a good idea for a movie — it's got a story twist that's really clever. The problem is you mention it three times in the entire script. That's what we're paying our money to see. Play the joke!

I was working with a writer who was writing a fun script and wouldn't commit to the joke: a talking dog who would insult people. It was funny. The dog's name was Lenny.

Wait a minute. We gotta hear what Lenny says when he insults everyone or we'll come after you with torches. That's the joke.

Five pages later:

Now I'm pissed. :) Another Lenny scene with no insults? Play the joke.

Another five pages later:

Now we're talking! The George Washington insult, I'm embarrassed to say, made me laugh out loud.

Later in the script:

He gives Lenny away? This worries me. Lenny is why I'm here. He better not be gone for long. Terrific work.

A writer I was working with was writing a movie where dating nightmare guys was the joke.

This can't be right. The 'A' story isn't going fast enough. We're almost fifty minutes in and she's been on only one date. We're here to see her try to solve her problems by dating. She has to have way more than one date at this point.

And to another writer I wrote:

We're sixty pages in and there aren't enough memorable scenes of levitation. It should be the bread and butter of this screenplay and I'm hard pressed to remember the memorable ones. It seems more about a guy getting high rather than levitation. The ending, unfortunately, doesn't involve the major joke of the script and ends on Vanessa, a character we have no stake in.

In this writer's screenplay, the joke is levitation. That's what this script has to sell. It's what the writer will pitch. It's what will be in the trailer and ad campaign. It's why this picture will get made if it does. It's incumbent on this writer to deliver the joke, to play it, so to speak, so we get our money's worth. This writer didn't and I felt ripped off. A violation of genre expectations. Scenes unrealized. Promises unmet. (*See* GENRE EXPECTATIONS)

positive reinforcement

I've included — and none too soon — the following section for you to read when you're down in the dumps and someone has told you your pages are only good for sopping up sour milk. Believe it or not, these are actual quotes from script notes I've given different screenwriters:

Real good pages. Keep it up.

It's been an exciting read. I'm really pleased, really. I particularly like that throughout you are keeping the visuals alive and reinforce what we see on the screen. Strong writing. Good going.

You nailed the ending. Terrific job!

Good work. I think your writing is really progressing. This script — really any script — takes a huge amount of work. I would urge you to keep at it, maturing the script, filling it in, maximizing. You've come a long way since the beginning of this unfocused idea — and you've some way to go. Stick to it.

I think this has some terrific stuff and is ripe for rewriting and expanding. It's a wonderful idea and your job now is to fully realize the idea, to reach the potential.

In my mind you're at the beginning of the process. Great idea, interesting characters with a lot yet to be realized.

Good work. Definitely worth continuing on. Ultimately, I think you can accomplish all that you want to and make it a readable, fun, entertaining and fabulously horrific and cutting-edge entertainment — it's just going to take some more work. What else is new?

Your script is flowing and is a good exciting read — I'm really pleased.

So when you're writing and the path ahead is overwhelming and you feel like giving it up and becoming a Barista at Starbucks, read the script notes above and pretend I'm talking about your script.

Feel better?

Good.

Now get back to work.

Iọ

questions to ask yourself

Here's a bunch of questions that you can ask yourself that will help you zero in on the things you need to be focused on when conceiving, writing, and re-writing your script.

Hopefully, the answers will better clarify what exactly you're doing.

What's the rating?
Who's the audience?
What movie is it like?
When it's finished, what do you want to do with this script?
What about this story makes you want to write it?
Who's the main character?
What's the main character's goal?
What does your main character do to accomplish his goal?
What obstacles are in his/her way?
What do you want us to feel about the main character?
What's his or her arc?
Is the main character in the center of your script?
How many drafts have you written on this?
What about this idea intrigues you?
Why should the studio invest in this project?
What's the hook? (I hate this question)
What's the 'A' story?
What's the 'B' story?
What's the 'C' story?

How do the 'B' and 'C' stories relate to the 'A' story?

Is the story open or closed?

What's the "joke" of the movie?

How many times do you play it?

How would you market this movie?

What are the trailer scenes?

Who's the antagonist?

What does he/she do?

What is his/her arc?

What story are you promising that makes me want to turn the page?

Why does the reader care?

What is the story you want to tell?

What is the log line?

R

resonance

I write to a writer whose script is all over the place.

I get a sense that scenes are not resonating. Jenny goes to church, but it never means anything to any other part of the script. Your script, unfortunately, is filled with isolated events like the one I describe above that don't build, don't evolve, don't feed on each other, in short, don't resonate with each other.

Story elements resonating is one of the things that makes scripts a satisfying read and a terrific movie. If scenes relate and evolve, the reader/viewer does what instinctively they want to do: put the elements together into a cohesive whole. That process is one of the major satisfactions in screenwriting.

A good way to achieve resonance in your script is to code your scene list to follow the different threads to see when and if they build into more satisfying wholes. Track the codes and make sure they have a build — Rising Action — and are close enough together in the script to provide a building narrative pull.

rewriting

```
Four red booths, a small bar with four regulars
throwing them back and a shuffleboard game.
```

**Not enough. Your job as screenwriter is to report what's
up on the screen so we can see it. Your default position
as a writer is to under describe your scenes. Describe
what you see.** (*See* DEFAULT POSITION AS A WRITER)

I was hired for a private consultation. I developed the script
with the writer, who was very talented. She did a first draft,
I gave her tons of notes, she executed them and sent me the
new draft to see "*if you have any notes before I send it to my
agent?*"

My notes were:
**You need to finish the script. Getting to FADE OUT
doesn't mean you're finished. You're just beginning.**

The cliché is true: WRITING IS REWRITING.

**My suggestion now that you've reached FADE OUT is
to have a glass of champagne, then go back and write a
new scene list based on the actuality of your pages, then
plot what you have to change, how you can improve the
script and what it needs. Once you have a strategy on
what your rewrite is — go for it. Keep writing and keep
thinking about writing.**

Here are my notes to another writer:

I like your screenplay. But, your work isn't done. You've done two drafts. Your job is to reach the potential of the idea and you're not close. I'd say you're sixty percent there. My guess is you feel you're ninety-eight percent there.

Two drafts ain't going to cut it. Writing is — in fact — rewriting. And for me, the bonus is, rewriting is fun. It's polishing the gem, making it perfect, realizing the potential of the idea and accomplishing that makes me feel good. Now get to work.

WHAT MAKES GREAT SCRIPTS?

Gone With The Wind — Six writers. Countless rewrites.

The Wizard of Oz — A dozen writers. Endless rewrites.

Citizen Kane — 250-page first draft. Five drafts to get to right length. Budget rewrites by Welles. Three new drafts by Joe Mankiewicz. A Hays Office (industry morals code board) rewrite. At least ten rewrites.

Casablanca — Based on a play. Two teams wrote drafts. Seven writers total.

When I first started reading and writing screenplays I thought that screenwriters wrote what I read right out of the chute. That it just came out perfectly the first time. I didn't know about rewrites and restructuring and working scenes to make them better, about developing threads and arcs and subplots and subtext. Then, I learned about rewriting and really became a writer.

The best analogy of rewriting I know is creating a piece of sculpture. Starting with a big chunk of raw marble, the sculptor's job is to find the sculpture in the stone, just as your job is to find the final script in the raw pages of your rough draft.

"Rewriting is the challenge of the Gods" says veteran TV scribe Deborah Dean Davis, writing in the *Writers Guild of America Journal.*

WHAT DOES REWRITING GET YOU?

Rewriting maximizes ideas.

Rewriting makes the story round and richer.

Rewriting brings rough-draft scene descriptions to life.

Rewriting raises characters from cardboard to memorable.

Rewriting evolves the important scenes from workmanlike to unforgettable.

Rewriting allows writing to mature, to season, to be perfected.

Rewriting facilitates making connections and resonances that deepen the screenplay.

Rewriting gives you a chance to perfect your script.

Rewriting increases your chances of selling your screenplay.

Rewriting makes your writing and the script better.

rhythm of your script

I wrote to one of my writers who was about to start his rewrite:

Examine the rhythm of your script. It feels as if there's no breath, no air between sequences — it's one thing right after another without giving the characters or the reader/viewer time to catch their breath. There's a storm, that's half a page, then something happens, then half a page, then something else happens. It all arcs and that is good, but it feels neverending, unrelentingly wall-to-wall. At one point, I wrote in your script "Enough."

Around 74 — it gets to be a little *Perils of Pauline*, in that everything happens to her and happens one right after another. Your new scene list should help examine the rhythms of your script. Your exciting scenes will play more exciting when they have contrasting scenes.

rising action

Most of the screenwriters in Hollywood have been brought up reading all the books that teach three-act structure as the structural motif for screenplays, with a formula for when inciting incidents and plot points and the like should occur.

Have a seat. This is going to take a second.

Screenwriting by formula has never made sense to me.

How can it be possible that every story is structured the same?

How can it be possible that the integrity of the story isn't violated because the formula tells you that on page twenty-four is where the inciting incident, or plot point, or hook, or whatever, belongs? I don't get it. It defies logic.

I believe each story has its own intrinsic integrity and the less formulaic strictures you impose on your story the better.

With that said, I'll get right to it: *the three-act structure is dead.*

I know it's going to make you nervous to be told that, but, as far as screenwriting is concerned, it's true. Stick a fork in it — the three-act structure is done. Three-act structure is old-fashioned, is antiquated, it's over. Say goodnight, Gracie. Three-act structure — I dance on your grave! Okay, okay, a little over the top, but I'm trying to make a point here.

Why have times changed? Theatre, literature and the guy on the corner aren't the only games in town doing the storytelling anymore — welcome to the world of a million cable TV options, thousands of films being made in virtually every country on this planet, storytellers uploading literally hundreds of thousands of hours of story each week on to YouTube and the Internet and their equivalents around the globe and this is just the beginning of Webisodes and video games grossing nearly four hundred million dollars the first three days of its release and on and on and on.

In this day of wall-to-wall media, the reader/viewer is so much more sophisticated than in the past, so much more used to seeing storytelling — on television, in commercials, on the Internet, in movies, in games, all day long — almost since the day they were born. It's our new skill set.

I was with an eighteen-month-old young man yesterday by the name of Jett Lazarus and he was carrying around his mother's iPhone and looking at videos, scrolling, finding the video he wanted to see and watching it and playing games. Eighteen months old!

What it means to me is we shouldn't be telling stories in the same way we did because our reader/viewer has changed.

The old formula:

A 30-page First Act — the introduction — setting up the characters and environment. That's what every book says. Well, not any more.

In the day and age where the three-act structure was relevant, there was a lot of introduction needed. The reader/viewer of old — before TV, movies and the Internet — was indeed being introduced to locales and characters that were not within their experience. Now, they get it. Everything is within everyone's experience. There are no longer restrictions of time, or distance or isolation. Everything is accessible. We can create anything. There are no limits. It's a changed world.

A 30-page Second Act, where the hero's journey begins and, at the end of the act, they hit bottom.

A 30-page Third Act where the hero rises to sweet victory.

Today, instead of needing 30 pages to set up the characters, the environment, and give the backstory, today we need three to five pages, ten pages at the most.

Why?

Because we get it.

Our reader/viewer lives in a world where the speed of editing has gotten so fast, the assault of the media — of stories — has gotten so all-pervasive and multifaceted that they get characters and get stories and it's become a much more shorthand world — a world of a hundred and forty characters — and your screenplay should reflect that.

The person who will watch your movie or the reader who evaluates your script gets it. So what replaces the recently deceased three-act structure?

There, as clouds part and the golden rays of sunlight filter down from the heavens is the replacement... RISING ACTION!

Rising Action is really very simple: THE MAIN ACTION OF YOUR STORY BECOMES *MORE AND MORE* AS YOUR SCRIPT EVOLVES.

That means if you're writing a love story — the main action of the love story starts with a look, evolves to a brush of the fingertips, then a fleeting kiss, an embrace, interrupted beginnings of passion, then, finally, intimacy. After that: unleashed passions, then even MORE AND MORE.

Each time you visit the main action of the story, it's building, you're giving the information-hungry reader/viewer MORE. If you don't give them more regularly, they get bored and put your script down.

If you're writing a movie about a serial killer: it starts with what seems like a random murder. Our hero investigates, then two people are killed. It's getting worse. Next, a member of the police force is murdered. A note is left. It's a serial killer. Then, a high-profile murder. The circle is getting tighter. Next, an attempt on the protagonist's life. The mystery and the stakes are increasing. It's now in his face — then, at the end, the confrontation, the final showdown: good vs. evil.

The action arcs up, rises; gives the reader/viewer MORE each time. The stakes and jeopardy increase as the story goes along.

MOVIE RECOMMENDATION

See a movie called *Stranger Than Fiction* — from screenwriter Zach Helm — it's the perfect example of RISING ACTION. After a brief introductory scene — what used to be a 30-page Act One — the story begins and then every few minutes new information is put into the mix — in other words, MORE AND MORE, and the movie just takes off.

The same Rising Action structural motif can be seen in a variety of different genres: *Iron Man* starts right up on page one and never lets up, and the wonderful Alan Pakula-directed *All The President's Men* has a real arc of rising action as well. And, of course, one of my favorite movies, writer John Patrick Shanley's *Moonstruck*, starts right away and keeps on going — complicating, rising, and being just wonderful.

road movies

I'm asked to read a lot of road movies. A lot. You know the kind of script: Three high school pals hook up on their last summer before college and drive around and have a series of episodic, wildly funny, beer-soaked, jiggly scenes.

Well, it ain't enough for me.

Why?

Because, as I've written about, the reader/viewer's nature is to find order in chaos; in other words, they want to start putting a story together, want to start adding up the different elements and putting together the pieces of the story puzzle. (*See* RESONANCE) When the story doesn't evolve in any meaningful way — is just a series of amusing scenes that don't go anywhere story-wise — well, it becomes tiring because the story doesn't naturally pull you along, doesn't invite you in, so the reading becomes labored. The experience of your script becomes muddled and you've lost your audience because there isn't content or character to hook into. This is not a good thing. (*See* NARRATIVE PULL)

So, if the movie you have in you is a road movie — then just don't settle on what your trip was like when you and your pals did the Vomit Tour of the National Parks two years ago. Make it more than those memorably funny scenes — make it interesting and human, with disclosure of information that makes us want to turn the page to find out what's happening next.

rules

Why would robots need to eat?
What if someone else drinks the elixir?
Is Lita the only person who can see the Wizard?
How many wishes can he grant?
What if someone other than Lola says the magic words?

All these notes address the same issue: if you have a joke that's what the movie is about, you have to play the joke as we've discussed, and, at the same time, also be very consistent with the use of it. As the writer, you have to know what the parameters and rules of your joke are and religiously stick to them.

It's a good idea before you write your script to write the rules out so you're totally consistent and true to them. When the reader/viewer feels the rules are arbitrary and have been developed to answer screenwriting issues as they arise, it gets sketchy. The reader/viewer should feel there's no question as to the internal logic of the joke.

A lot of times the joke evolves as you write it. It's always important to take a "joke pass" on your script to ensure the rules you've employed are consistent.

scene description

One of my student's default writing positions was to write lots and lots of scene description. The issue for me was that the writer described things GENERICALLY rather than SPECIFICALLY.

My script notes:

I believe on some level we all picture what's happening as we read a screenplay. The issue with your generic description is that I can't picture what's going on specifically. You write "Tree" rather than "Banyan Tree." With "Tree" I'm forced to fill in what I imagine versus you taking responsibility and describing the tree specifically.

My advice is to go through your script only focusing on scene description and revising it so it's specific.

TOO LITTLE SCENE DESCRIPTION

```
Diners in patron-style clothes.
```

And exactly what would "patron-style clothes" be? Way too minimal. Your job is make us see what you're writing about.

TOO MUCH SCENE DESCRIPTION

```
Louise is still wearing jeans, but now with a
very pretty top with a very low neckline and a
beautiful shell necklace around her neck.
Nervously touching her necklace, Louise looks
```

> around the café. The design resembles a typical
> New York bistro, and all the waiters wear long
> white aprons and crisp blue button-down shirts.
>
> Noisy youths in turtlenecks and baseball caps
> occupy several tables.

I'd like you to consider deleting every single word of that over-the-top scene description above. It is too dense and too detailed and too boy-I-don't-care-about-that-at-all. It slows down your script to a stop.

Another writer's work:

> Vanessa moves to Ginny's closet: there were
> sweaters, blouses, slacks hanging from pants
> hangers, boxes of shoes piled on the top shelf.
> On built-in shelves are folded jeans, and shorts
> and a number of plastic storage boxes with clear
> plastic covers.

Way, way too much meaningless detail. Do we really have to know what's hanging in the closet? Unless the murder weapon's going to be found in a purse in that closet, and I know it's not, please cut this meaningless and off-putting detail.

One of my student's default writing position highlights the issue of GENERIC DESCRIPTION versus SPECIFIC DESCRIPTION.

> Alma, in a dress, walks into the large room.
> It's filled with well-dressed people. Paintings
> are on the wall. MUSIC plays. She looks out the
> window to see the landscape.

Yikes. Could anything be dryer than that?

Here's a challenger:

> The land's endless enormity and indistinct
> geography make for challenging orientation.

Boy, I want to see that movie.

One of my students submitted his pages — including a conversation that spread over four pages — with NO SCENE DESCRIPTION — just dialogue.

Where are the visuals? You're writing radio.

He responded:

"The note that I'm writing radio doesn't influence me to change the Amy/Messina scene. It's an argument I hear, but Tarantino and Sorkin use long dialogue scenes constantly. And I'm NOT comparing myself to them; far from it. However, I feel like I'm providing a lot of visuals and action in the script in general, so this is a break in the action yet still provides intensity. I really like the scene the way it is. If there's a different reason I should change it, please let me know, but I find face to face dialogue scene confrontations just as exciting as action scene confrontations. I'm all ears."

Well, simply put, you're not Sorkin or Tarantino. I believe there's a different set of rules for them than for you and me.

One of my favorite scripts is *The Social Network*. Aaron Sorkin wrote the opening scene without scene description. He can — I don't think you should. Sorkin hands the script to producer Scott Rudin and the director David Fincher and it's an Aaron Sorkin script. Aaron Sorkin doesn't have to sell it. Tarantino the same. Their reputations and track records allow them certain courtesies and trust. You? Me? Not so much.

If I'm right and readers are put off by your lack of responsibility for images and the breaking of format expectations for three or four pages and pull them out of your script, what have you gained?

If I'm wrong and you put the scene description in, what do you lose? Frankly, I don't think it's going to make that much difference, but I do believe anything you do

that breaks normal format and calls attention to itself by its difference, takes readers out of your script and you don't want to do that.

One of my students wrote a very poetic scene description which, unfortunately, though beautifully wrought, called attention to itself and away from the script:

Nearby, a snowmobile patiently summers.

A little precious for my tastes, particularly as it's unimportant. When the reader comes across writing like "Nearby, a snowmobile patiently summers." it's so different I believe the reader pauses for just a moment — to think about what exactly that means, likes it — then moves on. *You've effectively taken the reader out of the script*. You do that enough, they spend too much time out of the script and it affects the read negatively.

Here are script notes to a writer who only wrote generic description:

I don't see much of your script. You don't describe what we see on the screen. I think you should show Belize by air — as the plane approaches. I think you should show the exterior of the beautiful and tropical Belize airport and name it by name.

I don't get a sense of South America. It should be accomplished with grace notes.

Laura's wearing a uniform. Does she have a virginal white blouse on covering her amazing body? Is she tanned and beautiful with a tight skirt? Does she weigh three hundred pounds? What color are her eyes? Is she bald?

What does the hotel suite look like? You have to describe more specifically than "well appointed." When she looks at the panorama — describe what she sees. The street vendor looks like what? Makes what kind

of drink? Take more responsibility for what the reader "sees." It's what screenwriting is all about.

I've mentioned the movie *Stranger Than Fiction*. If you see it again or for the first time, watch Dustin Hoffman and see how he is always doing something in the scenes. *In your scene description give your actors something to do.* The worst thing is to picture a movie where actors are standing around waiting for their turn to talk.

One of my online writers wrote a scene:

```
INT. DINER — NIGHT

A Couple, he's in overalls, she's in a flowered
dress, having burgers in a booth. At the
counter, a man nurses his coffee and cruller.
NANCY, the heavyweight Waitress, watches the TV,
on mute, in the Kitchen. The Special for the
Day, Marge's Meatloaf is under a metal screen
anti-fly dome next to…
```

Wait a minute! Wait a damned minute! The special is Marge's Meatloaf? Too much description. Lovely, but TOO MUCH DESCRIPTION. Yes, the screenwriter's job is to report what's on the screen, but, please, not the meatloaf.

The screenwriter has to prioritize the imagery, make some choices, communicate things that are story-relevant. A little color is all right but don't tell me what the special of the day is, please.

```
Paul enters a minimal, chic and crowded lounge.
Attractive people in stylish clothing drink
cocktails.
```

Yeah, but what do I see? What visuals can I take from the description? "Attractive?" "Stylish?" "Cocktails?" "Chic?" All too generic. This is probably a global note throughout your script and probably the default position of your writing — meaning that's the

way it comes out. That's something you should focus on in your rewrite.

Notes to another writer:

Your description, though there, is non-visual. "Rich but not extravagant." "Designer decorated." They could mean anything, therefore mean nothing. They aren't descriptions that can be pictured, they have to be imagined. You should take more responsibility and describe what we see on the screen. It's not about writing words on a page, screenwriting's about reporting what we see and hear on the screen. Please look back over the whole script and apply this note where pertinent.

And to another writer:

The description of the loft is better — but still not specific enough. "A mix of free spirit and NY chic." But what do I see? What does it LOOK like? It's not about words or writing — it's about describing.

scene list

Scene Lists are an important writer's tool. They give you a chance to conceptualize the scenes in the script in chronological order. Very minimal. Not spending time on prose and writing. Just thinking and listing.

Here's an example of a scene list for a script called *Carnal Innocence*.

The scenes in CAPS are flashbacks.

Meet Eric rowing on river.

He sees Dark-haired Woman walking.

ERIC AND HIS WIFE IN FIRE ISLAND — SEE YOUNG GIRL

Eric photo shoot of Clint Eastwood, sees Woman again.

ERIC WATCHES YOUNG GIRL

Eric searches for tape.

ERIC VIDEOS KIDS PLAYING

Eric finds tape. Looks at it.

YOUNG GIRL ON TAPE

YOUNG GIRL POSES FOR CAMERA

Eric watching tape. The Young Girl is the Dark Haired Woman.

Eric sees Dark Haired Woman when he rows.

ERIC TAPES YOUNG GIRL NAKED IN WATER

Dark Haired Woman comes to house. Meets Robin.
Talks with Eric. Eggs.

ERIC SHOOTS YOUNG GIRL NAKED AGAIN????

Robin thinks Eric should date Karen.

ERIC TALKS AND SHOOTS YOUNG GIRL. HAVE FUN. SHE
POSES.

Eric walks past Phillips House. No sign of
Karen. No sign of life.

ERIC AND LISA LEAVE FIRE ISLAND. GIRL WAVES FROM
DOCK.

Eric and Robin meet Karen in ice cream parlor.
Robin invites for dinner.

LISA ALMOST CATCHES ERIC LOOKING AT VIDEO OF
GIRL

Eric 'helps' Karen and Robin with dinner. R asks
Karen if married.

Eric shoots Karen through window.

Eric shoots Karen in studio. She touches self
like Young Girl.

ERIC AND LISA DECIDE TO GO TO FIRE ISLAND FOR
VACATION

Eric looks for Karen, finds her topless in hot
tub with Robin.

Karen explains to Eric that everything was
innocent.

And here's another example:

Hollywood Capone SCENE LIST

INTRO CAPONE IN CHICAGO

INTRO JOHNNY AS BAGMAN IN LA

CAPONE AND MAE ON TRAIN — INTEREST IN MOVIES

JOHNNY REPORTS TO BOSS LORENZO

CAPONE HAS FOOD TESTED

LORENZO GIVES JOHNNY ASSIGNMENT: BABYSIT CAPONE

CAPONE ARRIVES IN LA

JOHNNY MEETS CAPONE

JOHNNY SHOWS CAPONE AND WIFE HOTEL

JOHNNY REPORTS BACK TO LORENZO

LORENZO ORDERS OTHERS TO WATCH CAPONE

JOHNNY AND CAPONE GO TO BEACH

COPS FOLLOW

BIG CHASE

JOHNNY LOVES BEING WITH CAPONE

JOHNNY TAKES CAPONE TO MEET LORENZO ON BOAT

LORENZO OFFENDS CAPONE, WHO SUCKS IT UP

JOHNNY TAKES CAPONE TO MGM

Simple, fast, conceptual — the most efficient way to conceive a movie.

(*See* BEGINNING YOUR SCREENPLAY)

scenes you don't write

One of the more interesting issues I run into.

I wrote to one of my students:

Frank's in jail!?! What the hell? Wait a minute, Roberto, you're not writing the big scenes. Where's the arrest? The chase? I don't get it. Those are the trailer scenes — the best scenes in your script that would appear in the trailer for the movie.

And to another writer:

Kim, you mean we don't see the scene where Lena sticks a knife in Rick's neck and escapes?!?! That's the only action in the first thirty pages and the first time Lena finally stands up for herself — and you don't show us the scene? This is where I'd put the script down. Please go back and write that scene. Write it as long as you want. It's the heart of your screenplay.

And to another writer:

We didn't see the aftermath of the accident where Cary and the others decide to look for Cristina. We're missing the important scenes. Please take a look at this.

And another:

Where's the fight? You've built to this fight for fifty pages and you cut away before the end of the fight. It is common for writers not to write the big scene which is clearly what you've done now a number of times. It's as if the script for *The Diary of Anne Frank* focused on the re-decorating of the attic.

I can't tell you how many scripts I've read that build to the key scene, and then amazingly the writer doesn't write it. When I think about it, it's totally logical. This is the big scene. It's a little crazy-making so they just pass it by. My guess is they're not even aware of it. I mean it's hard enough to write a good script. Writers put pressure on themselves to perform, to write the perfect script, the big scene. And the biggest scenes are the scariest to write. The deal is: write it. Never back down on those big scenes. Never back down when you hit the wall, when you run dry. Just keep writing. Keep moving forward. If you keep working, it will come.

I was working with a writer whose default style was to leave a scene too early, robbing us of the pleasure of watching it, so he could reveal in the next scene the result of what happened. Not satisfying to read or see at all.

I wrote him:

I think you're missing some of the best and hardest to write scenes as Reggie orients himself. He sees a girl from last night sleeping under the covers in the bed next to him. He cringes and slowly lifts the sheet to have a look. She's naked. The problem for me is we've missed the important stuff: when he meets the girl and takes her back to the room. How did that happen? Did Leo set him up? Was she the aggressor? Did he sleep with her? Was he drunk or not? That could be fifteen pages — never written.

One of my consultation's script:

```
Sarah and Mr. Dodd are standing outside her
hotel room door. He kisses her forehead. They
are still holding hands. They look tired but
happy.

CLOSE UP on Sarah and Dodd's hands as they part
while she enters her room.
```

This is the most emotional part of the movie and they don't speak. Please write what they would say to each other when they say goodbye. Take another pass and maximize every moment in this scene. Try it. What do you have to lose? If it doesn't work for you, trash it.

To another writer I wrote:
Brian slugs Roy then what happens? You cut away when things get interesting. Who rushes in? How does Roy react? How does Marcus react? This is the good stuff of your movie — write it!

This script was about a reality show. Just when the characters get into a major conflict, the writer cuts away.

I asked him why?

He said he didn't want it to be *"Over the top."*

I've done a lot of TV. The studio execs — rightfully so — would be thrilled at that kind of fight on camera. That's where they get their ratings. Over the top isn't all bad.

The reason screenwriters don't write the big scene?
Fear.

It's something you should take a look for in your scripts. Make sure you deliver the goods in the big scenes.

If you want a little more on what to do when you hit the wall, go to TOMLAZARUS.COM and read my interview with 'A' writer Scott Frank, one of the best writers in Hollywood. See how he deals with hitting the wall.

script consultants

A screenwriter reached out to me online:

"I have sent this story to several script consultants, and they all say different things. The only thing everyone seems to agree on is that it's funny, but everyone has a different suggestion on where to take this story. I want to listen to what everyone is suggesting, but find it has hindered the process more than it's helped. After reading your book, Secrets of Film Writing, *I realized this is a common problem even for seasoned writers like you. How do you filter what everyone says but remain open to the expert's suggestions?"*

I'd start by stop listening to every Tom, Dick, and Harry. It's okay to get feedback. It's necessary. But, it's not easy. I see it in my classes. The other students give notes and the writer whose script it is hears ten sets of notes and doesn't know which end is up.

The deal is: you have to get in touch with your gut. This is your script. You have to protect it, you have to be the person who matures this script, and you have to decide what's best for it.

Listen to the notes, then listen to yourself. You've seen a million movies, you have a sense you know what you're writing about. You're the last word on your script.

The great thing about writing — it's rewriting, so you're going to have a chance to re-visit the decision. Say thank you for the notes. Consider them. Make up your

mind. Try them. And if they don't work, change them. No big deal. It's a process.

As for script consultants — if you're going to go to a script consultant, do your homework:

Ask the consultant exactly what services they perform and for what price.

Ask them for a sample of the service you're asking them for.

Do your due diligence: interview a couple of consultants. Look at their credits, their experience, ask what kind of movies they like, see if you're simpatico, if you like their vibe.

And when you get your notes from the consultant, ask questions. You've paid them, get your money's worth.

script notes

Here are some samples of my script notes in full, not just excerpts. You'll see some of what I mention in other sections in the book, but they're complete and give you an idea of script notes in context.

> **Notes for Hank**
>
> **Whenever you change locations it has to be a new scene.**
>
> **Skip another line before each scene for easy reading.**
>
> **A three-minute flashback of old France — what does it get you?**
>
> **"Like he ate a bug" — an image that doesn't appear on screen.**
>
> **Anything written on screen should be <u>underlined</u>.**
>
> **The tourists are funny — for those who know Yiddish. What percentage of the reader/viewers — or, for that matter, your audience — knows Yiddish?**
>
> **"Flush on the river?" Meaning? Don't have your writing call attention to itself.**
>
> **Whenever you change locations it has to be a new scene. This is a global note — which means you should check your whole script for this.**
>
> **What make of car? Be specific so we have an image in our brains.**

So, I'm 12 pages in and have no idea what the movie is about — not a good thing.

The flashback to ancient Mesopotamia gets you what? For me, it doesn't move the story and postpones any reader/viewer involvement.

Notes to another writer:
Hey Mark -
I really like a lot of things in this script: the characters are terrific but could be delineated a little better. Easy to fix.

The big issue for me is you're trying to tell too many stories. This piece needs some narrative pull — a stronger spine, a more recognizable 'A' story. You need to choose what story is your main story and let that have a narrative pull, making us turn the page. Otherwise, there's a flatness about it that discourages emotional/psychological/story investment from your reader/viewer. You can accomplish the same kind of storytelling by re-weighting your stories a bit.

My suggestion for the next step — after your log line and scene list — is to list the many stories and then prioritize them. After that, I'd like us to talk specifically about the rewrite, starting with revising your newly created scene list.

You've created a really interesting world. Keep writing and keep thinking about writing. Good work.

And to another writer whose script was all over the place:
Hi Anne Marie —
Individual scenes are really well written and I have no technical/craft issues at all. But, and it's a big but, this screenplay is in desperate need of a narrative line — an 'A' story if you will — to pull us through it. Right now, you set up your storylines: Rita/Lita, the Friedmans, Randy, Jennifer, Lars, Lars Jr., the Board of Education,

Fredric and his partner Cedric and their dog Hendrick, and that's just off the top of my head — and you're still introducing new characters around page 50.

From the very beginning, you have to decide what story is most important because that's the story you have to start devoting pages to. My guess is the Rita/Lita and Fredric/Cedric stories are the richest. Work with your scene list to see where you can add onto those narrative lines.

All of your existing story arcs evolve too slowly. The Randy/Jennifer scenes are basically all the same. ALL THE THREADS SHOULD IMPACT ON THE 'A' STORY. Now they're separate.

The sameness note is true with a lot of the storylines. Make the arcs longer, prioritize them, building up the 'A' story a lot.

My suggestion at this point is: you have this draft — put it aside. You can always come back to it. Then construct a new scene list with the 'A' story only — just the main story, and crank it up.

Maybe you should start revealing the machinations of the 'A' story and disclose it throughout as a way of sucking us in. I'd seriously consider this last note.

Here's another longer script note:
The way the characters are introduced makes it too hard to figure out who is who. Is Silas the boss? We meet his wife first. Hard to discern.

Don't know who I'm supposed to follow in terms of a main character or what the story is yet.

Why don't we see the Greenlee brothers' audacious robbery? Sounds cinematic.

How do we know we're flashing back 24 hours? And why do it this way? When we cut to across the city, are we still in flashback? I like the TV connection seeing the victims in the car. Nice.

Well, I finished the treatment and don't know who the main character is and what the story is. The test for me — and I've read it three times — is can I pitch the story — do I know enough to tell it?
The answer?
No.

I'm not sure what you're gaining — other than confusion — by the jumping of time. It seems as though you don't trust the story enough to present it linearly. Confusion on the part of the reader is death. Your job is to make it accessible, to seduce the reader into getting inside your story. These pages, unfortunately, do the opposite.

My advice is to work on writing the piece linearly and longer, more detailed. I would work on identifying the characters more completely, individualizing them — so that they'd be easier for the reader to identify. And maybe most important: you should be telling story through the main character. We access the script through the main character — it's who we root for.

Who's the main character and what's his journey?

I think if you do the above mentioned rewrites, you'll at least give your story a fighting chance.

I give script notes to writers in Great Britain through Circalit, an online screenwriters site, and here's one of them.

The strategy of teasing why these characters are going on their road trip to London for fifty pages may not be serving you as there's a deep sag where the story treads water for way too long in the second act.

If you had allowed the reader/viewer to have a greater stake in the story earlier by letting us in on what was happening with the characters, it would have been much easier to hook into the story.

The Good News? *Make Me A Malted* has all the ingredients for a terrific script — good entertaining characters we like and root for, sometimes great dialogue, and a few surprises. It's good writing and a pleasure to read.

The Bad News? The screenplay feels a bit underbaked. It needs a few more drafts, some sharpening of the rhythm and flow — there's an 11-page scene?!? — making the tone more consistent, and lessening the blood and violence in what essentially is a romantic comedy. The additional drafts will help the natural maturing and rounding out that comes with re-writing. You also need to focus on the final ten pages. Do all that and this is going to be a good, tight, marketable script.

Notes to another writer:

Hey Lacy –
Pages 1 and 2. Bookends — a scene from later in the movie as a device to hook the audience — are way overrated and some times defuse the climax. I think that's what the case is here.

Scenes 1 through 23: all set-up, all backstory. None of it involves your lead actress and the character — mature Ruth — you're going to ask the reader/viewer to invest in — nor what you profess to be writing about. In addition, many of the scenes are redundant. How many scenes do you have with young Ruth saying I'm going to be a star? I'm not sure you need or want any of these pages.

Take a deep breath. I think you're writing two stories: the story of young Ruth's career as a singer and the story of a singer who becomes a doctor and the incredible and terrific drama that ensues.

I think the first story — pages 1–24 — is just backstory. I think you should start the script around 24 and then have to focus more clearly on the story you want to tell.

For me, the story really kicks in around scene 70 when Ruth becomes an intern.

I think you've spent way too much time setting up and not nearly enough time telling the best parts of this story.

The story of the Hospital trying to get her to lie, the coercion, her defiance and strength, are the heart of this story. I think you've seriously shortchanged the end of the script.

This is the final scene of Lacy's scene list:

> Father secretly submits Ruth's songs to the London Music Awards. Ruth wins 2 awards and she starts to touring across the country and around the world to Basque communities with her completed CD in a tour bus newly renovated by her dad, and whole family. Ruth asks her Mother to be her manager and she agrees. End.

That "Army takes the town" scene could be twenty pages — the successful end to her story and not just one scene. You have more than enough story, actually way more than enough, so you're going to have to winnow down the size of what you're telling.

And my script notes to another writer:
This is much better. With that said, I'd like you to go back and rewrite these pages again — and this time, I'd like you to write their love/attraction arcing throughout the pages so that we can see their attraction grow.

My recommendation to you is to take a step back and re-conceive this script: same story, same characters, but thinking of it in terms of scenes where things happen, versus scenes where people talk about things happening. It's going to twist your head a little to make that leap. And it's not a play. You don't have to stay in one location. It's the exact opposite.

Your job is to seduce the reader/viewer, get them into your story and never let them go. What that means is you need a strong spine that is providing narrative pull. At the moment, you don't have it.

I should be able to know what the story is — I don't. You're just riffing.

Professionals in this business can tell by page one if the writer is any good, page five if the screenplay is worth reading, and page ten if they should put the script down and have an assistant read it.

And notes for another writer:
Hi Paul -
I like a lot of the writing. I'm not sure you have enough story or incident, or development of story.

You have to start digging deeper and fleshing this story out and making more out of James and Lucy's relationship — which is so smooth and uneventful that it's unnerving.

You have a habit of writing "just then..." and "all of a sudden..." Not needed. We know the next thing that happens happens all of a sudden or just then. Extra words, extra work.

sell it

A student submitted a horror script and the idea was really good. I've read and written a bunch of horror scripts and this had some nice, fresh twists in it. Characters doing surprising things, the story making twists and turns that were unexpected. All good.

The bad? The script was flat. So flat. Everything just lay on the page.

My notes:

Okay, here it is: you have too much action and not enough foreplay. No suspense, no creeping, creeping, waiting for something to jump out of the darkness. Don't go down that stairway! Don't go in there! Something... building... slowly... excruciating... jumping out of your skin waiting for something to happen.

Many times in the script, I note for you to write "more." You have to make the important story moments more important. You have to sell harder, write more detailed, give it more space on the page. Sell it, Baby, sell it!

My advice is for you to really go beyond what you think is over the top. You need to push yourself and get into the center of the script. You have to get into these scenes and mine them, find where the moments of suspense, of horror are — then write them as someone else.

You have to transcend your natural reticence and not worry what people are going to think. It's appropriate for you to have maggots eating eyeballs. It's okay. It's what's called for.

It took two more drafts, but finally the writer had maggots eating eyeballs. My work here was done.

set-up

A scriptwriter I was working with wrote a first act that was almost totally backstory: the main character as a small child, a few years older, in high school and then college. Three or four different kid actors, characters who don't return to the script. The script was about what happened to this character after being forced to move from her family's plantation as a young woman.

My script notes:

The first act is almost totally backstory. All that happens before the 'A' story kicks in. It involves characters we never see in the body of the script, incidents that don't resonate later and information that never plays again. My advice is to re-boot the structure.

What you have as Act II is really where the script should begin. Most of the information and scenes in your Act I are irrelevant. If you do need any of it, you can feather it in as you tell the 'A' story.

And the writer wrote me back:

"In addition to trimming the scenes, I need the scenes in the first act to really set up the theme of the movie."

No, actually, you don't. The theme of the movie should come out. It's inherent in your script and you don't have to do anything to set it up or talk about. Your theme should be subtext rather than text. No character should articulate the theme.

THE LAST WORD ■ LAZARUS

And the writer emailed me back.

"Doesn't a good movie do both set-up and give 'useful' information that we use throughout the movie?"

Actually, no. That's the way good movies and scripts used to be. The standard, old-fashioned, out-of-date, smelly old fish of the three-act structure takes too long to get going. Ideally, the first act — if you need to think that way — should be five to ten pages long. (*See* RISING ACTION)

I hate set-up. Like exposition, it's usually unneeded. Following is the beginning of a writer's scene list:

```
Scene One — The character announces he's going
to his lover's house.

Scene Two — The character arrives at his lover's
house.
```

Well, you don't need the first scene. You don't need to announce anything — just go to the lover's house. When we see the character arrive, we either know it's her house because we've seen it before, or we don't and after he knocks, who answers the door is a mystery. Either way, it's better than having a mind-sapping set-up scene.

That's an example that can be utilized on a lot of different levels. It's something to look for: unnecessary scenes — I'd like an appointment with Dr. Freud, please — that set up other scenes — Why, Dr. Freud, good afternoon! — unnecessary dialogue that sets up something to come rather than just letting it happen.

Don't set up dialogue, don't set up story points, don't set up behavior, don't set up anything. Let it all be a surprise, an adventure. That's why we love movies.

And to another writer:
Well, I'm not a big fan of set-up scenes. I'd rather you get the story going faster, much faster, and we learn

about the character as the story progresses — like he's a lawyer, he broke up with his girl — as the story meets them logically.

Fuzzy sets up the boys going to town for drinking and pool. And then you cut to the boys going to town for drinking and pool. A perfect example of what not to do. Why set it up, then show it? It takes the surprise and the newness out of the cut. Cut right to it.

IF YOU ABSOLUTELY NEED TO INCLUDE BACKSTORY

Okay, there are some scripts where including backstory is necessary. My advice is don't lead with it. Get your story going. Make sure your reader/viewer is hooked into your story, then run the backstory.

shocking!

I was working with a writer who submitted a script that was abusive to read — in the extreme.

I don't know about the tonality of your script which, as you know, includes: violent anal sex, cruelty to animals, meanness, vomiting — numerous times, bestiality, a camel taking a dump, the bleaching of orifices, sex with vegetables, slipping and falling in puke and on and on. I'm assuming it's an X. Plus, I'm not sure the most desirable way to introduce the main character is covered with menstrual discharge.

Actresses lining up to play that role, are they? Have you seen many movies like this? Who's the audience?

And then to another writer:
Why have your main character vomit *three* times? What do you get? What actor wants to do that?

This is in response to a general trend I've noticed in contemporary movies which is characters promiscuously vomiting — projectile and otherwise. I don't get it. Is there a lot of that going around? Am I missing something? This revulsion with wall-to-wall barfing might be idiosyncratic to me, if it is, please ignore this.

BREAKING NEWS!
I saw the Steve Carell and Tina Fey movie *Date Night* last night. I lasted about twenty minutes before I turned it off because I

realized I didn't care. In any event, there's a Steve Carell-pukes-three-times scene. I still didn't get it. You could have cut the footage out and it wouldn't have made a bit of difference to the story, but they didn't.

If you have any insights as to what's going on here, email me at the Vomit Hotline: LAZARUSTOM@AOL.COM. Thank you for your patience in regard to this matter.

Another writer wrote in their script:

    "...begins to masturbate..."

Really?

And then more vomiting:
Vomiting, huh? Lot of that goin' around. I wonder what the deal is. I guess it's just me that doesn't find it entertaining. Never mind.

Lots of masturbation:

    Our hero masturbates in the tub.

Really? Masturbation in movies is a lot like computers in movies: we all do it but does it make a good movie?

Women masturbate in scripts as well.
My note to the writer:
We learn nothing new about the main character in her masturbation scene other than she likes to put her fingers in her vagina and, if you pardon the word play, it's a bit self-serving. Lose it, please, then, after you sell the script, put it in the rewrite, okay?

Every once in a while I get an over-the-top, dirtiest-script-ever-written script: all in fun with lots of use of the F-Bomb, C-Word, Mother-F'er, C-Sucker, and even a few I haven't heard of. It's the texture of the movie. My notes about one such script:

I have a feeling that the early-on grossness, which, by the way, is truly gross, is pretty much unneeded. Once the script gets going — about page twenty — it works on an acceptable level. Tone down the opening and it might work a lot better for people you might want to buy this script. I think the challenge for this script is to make it a non-turn-off. It has to be something someone wants to invest five to twenty million dollars in. Too many "Pee pees and wee wees," as Bookman memorably says on *Seinfeld*, is problematic.

showing rather than telling

One of the foundations of screenwriting. Show rather than tell. It's not about dialogue, it's about images. It's about moving pictures. Motion. Action. Behavior. You don't want people to talk about it — you want them to do it.

Show rather than tell.

Print it out and stick it on your monitor.

I wrote to a student:

Why don't you show us this rather than have them talking about it? That's the next stage your writing has to get to — to write scenes that aren't about people talking — but rather doing.

Sometimes I get a little annoyed:

"STOP HAVING PEOPLE TALKING SO MUCH!!!!!"

It's a very common problem.

Let the actors act. WRITE ACTION. NOT TALK.

Look through your script. Make sure you're not telling the story to the reader. Make sure your characters are moving through your story doing things, not just talking about them. I'm trying to say it a bunch of different ways because it's so vital that you get it.

■ EXERCISE 15 — THE LAST WORD ON SHOWING RATHER THAN TELLING.

Take a scene in your screenplay and see if you can cut the dialogue and show the information cinematically.

slow motion

I'm never sure of the use of slow motion in scripts. It's clearly a cliché — but worse, it's also clearly not the writer's call. It's the director and the editor when they're working with the footage. In scripts it always feels too manipulative — and incredibly obvious.

If you succumb to the siren's call of slow motion, here's how you do it.

```
INT. PUPUSERIA — DAY
Jose levels his gun and fires!

SLOW MOTION OF BULLET
Spinning through the air and exploding into
Hector's head!

INT. PUPUSERIA — DAY — CONTINUOUS
Hector crumples lifelessly to the ground.
```

Whenever you use SLOW MOTION in a script it should be capitalized as it's an optical treatment.

I was working with a writer who came up with a great idea for a scene:

I love the stuff about being able to mentally ignite fires. Really good. The tension's there, I was totally into it, then you threw it into slow motion, distancing us suddenly from the reality and making it film versus something authentic and in the moment. The slow motion distances us from the tension because it suspends it. Try it without it and see how it reads to you.

smash cut

An almost meaningless expression in scripts and a sometimes effective film device. SMASH CUT signifies a jarring cut. On film it works, on the script page — not so much.

speaking out loud

The Screenwriter's main character, alone in her bedroom, walks to the window:

>   MAIN CHARACTER
>   Why is it that every man I date is
>   shaped like a gourd?

Who is she talking to? The only people in the room are the camera crew, the hack director, and the stoned soundman. The writer, as usual, isn't welcome on this set.

Do you walk into an empty room and ask questions? Who does this? Writers should find other ways to communicate their ideas. Asking actors to talk out loud is bad movie.

Yes, it's done a lot. That doesn't make it good. Don't you find yourself, as I do, asking: Who's he/she talking to?!

Another screenwriter wrote:

>   Victor is alone on the porch.
>
>   VICTOR
>   (PENSIVELY)
>   How should I bargain without knowing
>   what's inside?

And about five pages later, after Victor exits the house — alone:

>   VICTOR
>   I'd better keep this gizmo to myself.

I wrote to the writer:

I believe characters talking to themselves out loud is unrealistic and too easy. Work harder. You don't need any of the dialogue. Have his behavior tell us all.

The perfect example of a movie where the characters prattle on endlessly when they're alone is Nancy Meyers' truly awful *The Holiday*, with Cameron Diaz and Kate Winslet. Early on the characters start talking aloud when they're alone and I couldn't believe it. It continued, scene after scene, until I was shouting at the screen and had to be helped from the theater.

splintering time

One of my screenwriters submitted a script for my rewrite work-shop. For no apparent story reason, the writer had chosen to splinter the time and bounced from scene to scene, jumping forward in time, flashing back, and then, if that wasn't enough, he threw in dreams and "mind flashes" as well.

I wanted to throw the script out the window, but instead I took a deep breath and wrote these script notes:

I'm not sure what you're gaining — other than confusion and my wrath — by the jumping of time. It seems as though you don't trust the story enough to present it linearly.

Your job is to make your script accessible, to seduce the reader into getting inside your story. These pages, unfortunately, do the opposite. *My advice is to work on writing the piece linearly and longer, more detailed.*

And to another writer who seems to jump time almost at will:
Because the scenes are all splintered time-wise, there's no orderly logic to my emotional journey in trying to hook into the story. What is the splintered time getting you? Feels to me that you don't trust the heart of the material because you keep obfuscating it.

And to another writer:
My feeling is that all of that — the jumping of time, of putting everything in flashback or memory or re-creation — showing things that have happened robs

them of their spontaneity, their immediacy, and may work intellectually, but get in the way of connecting emotionally with the main character. Please consider this. I think your script is terminally flawed otherwise.

As part of our deal with the reader, we should be making the screenplay as easy to read and understand as we can, so that readers can access the material and get to the movie you want them to be watching. If your reader doesn't know what's going on and can't find anything to hold onto, then you lose them.

For anyone planning to splinter time — and I know you're out there — my suggestion is do a scene list of your script laid out linearly. See how it reads. See if now that you're not paying attention to the structure, you have a chance to access the characters and the story more emotionally. If it sucks linearly, burn the pages and move on.

I know there are some screenplays that are as much about the structure as story and that's the screenwriter's intent. *Traffic* and *Syriana* come to mind. It's clear my bias favors emotional accessibility to structural creativity. Like much in screenwriting, there's no one right way. The last word is: Does it engage the reader/viewer?

starting your screenplay fast

The first page is the most important page in your script.

The second page the second most important, and so on.

If your script isn't happening by page three — you're in trouble. If you're still jerking around by page five — well, don't give up your day job.

I wrote to one of the writers I was working with:

I went back and read your log line. Rita battles zombies. We're 23 pages in and we haven't met any zombies. What's the deal? It's all happening too slowly. As your next assignment I'd like you to consider drastically cutting down the first 23 pages so they're something like 5 or 7 pages. Try it and see if it works. If it does read great, as I suspect it will, rewrite accordingly.

My notes to another writer:

Well, your characters finally get together — unfortunately it's way too late. The love affair begins on page 37. If that's what you're writing about — and that's your log line — move it up as far forward as you can. Page 15 is a good target.

The writer wrote me back.

"How do I go about cutting more than 50% of the pages?"

Prioritize all the scenes that come before this on a scale of one to ten in terms of importance to the overall

movie, then keep cutting out the less important ones until you get down to page 15.

Notes for another writer:
We're an hour into this script and Loren is still having to convince the other characters that there's something wrong. We got it fifty-five pages ago. This script is treading water and not moving forward.

And another:
We're six pages in and no story has started. It's all introducing the characters. Not enough. I think you should be introducing your characters as the story progresses. Just introducing characters is not enough to carry the scenes at the beginning of the script.

And another:
I'd like you to reconsider the opening scene — not opening on the bad guys, but opening on Michael. This will be a continuing note that Michael is not front and center enough for our hero.

And:
You're opening on two scenes — five pages — with the grandparents which I don't understand because they are minor characters at best. Why aren't you starting with the 'A' story?

And to another writer:
You're fourteen pages in and you haven't taken responsibility as the writer to tell the reader/viewer what your script is about. Get to it!

And to another:
I'm on page ten, I think you have to start giving the reader a chance to start putting the story together or you will lose them. (*See* RESONANCE)

And one last one:

So, I'm nine pages in and Sid and Kathie are getting to know each other. No big drama. No big scenes. Just getting to know each other. Neither has a heavy passion or obsession. It's all very calm. You better get them in action pretty soon or we're going to stop reading this script.

You can't write the first ten pages of your script enough. They have to be perfect.

Actually, the same is true for the last ten pages. There is a tendency when getting to the end of your draft to "run to the barn" as writers. Write those last ten pages a lot. Draft after draft. You want to leave the reader with the best you can do. Just like the opening. Perfect. (*See* PERFECTIONISM)

structure

I understand the obsession with structure. It's a security blanket for many writers. And rightfully so. If someone tells some writers that on page 23 is where the inciting incident should be and on page 27 is where the protagonist meets Obstacle 2 and changes course, well, I guess that's one way to write a script. It takes the writer off the hook as to when things happen in their story. It all fits into a formula.

Frankly, thinking like that makes my head explode.

I'm a much more intuitive writer than that. I start writing the story and pretty soon the story itself begins generating the energy as well as the story logic. The story has its own integrity, it has its own structure, and, after a while, its own life. It's my job to recognize and honor it.

As long as the overall arcing motif is Rising Action so the reader/viewer is always given more as the story progresses, let the story tell itself. Let it tell you where it should be going. Let it come from inside you. Your solutions to the story. Your ideas. Your timing.

Writing a good, authentic story isn't about conforming to a pre-existing formula. It's about listening to your gut and solving the character and story issues in a fresh and creative way.

Those uncomfortable with that creative freedom can always structure according to formula.

If you want an act structure — I'd like you to think about using an eight-act structure, which mirrors the structural motif of television movies. Lots of little acts with beginning and middles and ends to leave room for commercials. Our viewing habits are used to that kind of series of scenes and you can do worse than having seven mini-climaxes before reaching your final climax. (*See* RISING ACTION)

I T

the deal

I had a writer who opened her script with a dream. She had fantasies, mind flashes, any number of different film languages. It didn't work for me.

I've mentioned The Screenwriter/Reader Deal before. This is what I wrote her:

> **There's a fragile unspoken deal between you, the screenwriter, and your reader. It's an understanding that you're on the same side, that you won't trick, embarrass, or in any other way screw around with their feelings. When you violate the terms of the deal — the reader falls away from your script and you've lost as your script goes into the Great Maw of Silence, never to be spoken about again.**
>
> **Dream sequences push at the relationship — events that happen in the script, then turn out to be fantasies. For example, you read a scene where the main character finally has had enough and kills his mother. It's gruesome. It goes on for a page and a half, then, and only then, at the end of the page and half, do you the writer reveal that it's baloney, it's a dream. I've gone through the emotional wringer about the matricide, felt for the main character's crisis, only to be betrayed by the writer. I lose trust. The next time there's a big dramatic scene, I wait for it to be a dream so I'm not as committed and it turns out this time it isn't a dream.**

The result? I'm out of the script and thinking about issues I shouldn't be.

The Screenwriter/Reader deal has been broken.

theme

A student wrote me:

"I can't show the painting in the opening sequence because this will confuse the audience who won't know about the underlying theme of why this sequence is important."

No, it won't confuse the audience. I'd rather the reader/ viewer have something to figure out — and it's not a good idea to open with a scene about underlying themes. The reader/viewer should discover this as they read/see the movie.

Just so you know where I'm coming from: I don't worry so much about theme. I'm a storyteller. I worry about the story and characters and giving the reader/viewer a hundred and ten minutes of something they haven't experienced before.

I'm not sure wrestling with theme enters into writing for Hollywood or writing assignments for television.

I'm not sure people go to movies because of the theme of the movie.

I usually discover what I'm writing about — theme — as I write. The theme seeps out.

On the final rewrite of this book, I realized the theme:

This book is about how to keep the readers engaged in your script.

the journey

Claire was a writer I was working with who brought in a screenplay that was all over the place. She did a couple of drafts and the script was improving. I'd talked long and hard about screenwriting being a process, but she lost confidence and lost her way.

> **Claire —**
>
> **I'm not sure why you feel lost. You've taken an unfocused screenplay and found the spine and are beginning to get it into shape. You've rewritten forty pages. They're working. What's the problem?**
>
> **Writing a screenplay takes work and takes time. You have to discover the writing by writing. I understand your impatience. The only way to solve it — is writing. That's what it's about. It's a process and you have to allow the process to go through its machinations. It's a journey of discovery. You have to allow yourself to NOT KNOW before you know. It's hard. If it were easy, it wouldn't be any fun.**

the scene — format

"A ribbon of dreams."

— Orson Welles, director of *Citizen Kane*, describing film

A screenplay is comprised of scenes.
The screenwriter tells his or her story scene by scene.
One scene after another.
From beginning to end.
A cinematic ribbon of scenes.

Here's the opening of a script:

RACE OF LIFE

Written by Tom Lazarus

```
FADE IN:

EXT. COUNTRYSIDE — NIGHT
FLYING TOWARD a sparkling jewel in the rural
landscape — a giant sign illuminated by towering
lights reads FREEDOM RACEWAY.

EXT. RACE TRACK — NIGHT

In front of a wildly CHEERING sell-out crowd,
two huge, lethal motorcycles — one black, one
red, side by side — race dangerously around the
oval and thunder for the finish line.

The Official waves his checked flag as the
black motorcycle just noses over the finish line
before the red.
```

```
EXT. PIT AREA — NIGHT
DARREN, in skin tight red leathers, a handsome,
buffed out blonde thirty years old, power slides
to a TIRE SCREECHING stop and jumps off the red
motorcycle.

                    DARREN
                 (sarcastic)
            Real cute.

He whips off his helmet…

                    DARREN
                 (continued)
            Cheating scum!

…and rushes BULLETS, six feet of evil in black
leather, who drops his black bike and heaves his
helmet at Darren.

                    BULLETS
            Loser!

Bullets is thrown a tire iron from the crowd as
Darren runs toward him.

Darren stops and they face each other — the big
moment has arrived.
```

Okay let's analyze these three scenes:

**Some nice white space at the top — to lighten the look
of the page.**

```
                    RACE OF LIFE
```

**Put the title on page one as well as on the title page.
Many times scripts lose the cover page.**

```
            Written by Tom Lazarus
```

Don't forget your name. You want the credit.

```
FADE IN:
```

**Every script starts with FADE IN. Even if it's a black
screen opening.**

```
EXT. COUNTRYSIDE — NIGHT
```
Every scene starts with a SLUG LINE and it's always comprised of three elements:
1. The physical location: EXT. meaning EXTERIOR is a scene out of doors.
    INT. means INTERIOR and the scene takes place inside.
    EXT./INT. means it takes place in both locations.
2. The actual location: COUNTRYSIDE. Every time you change locations, you change scenes.
3. And finally, NIGHT or DAY. More information as to what the scene looks like.

```
FLYING TOWARD a sparkling jewel in the rural
landscape — a giant sign illuminated against the
threatening sky reads FREEDOM RACEWAY.
```

The opening of a script is one of the very few times you get to be cinematic. Let the first shot be real "movie." When you do call a shot — like FLYING TOWARD — it should be capitalized.

NOTE: The last word on rules is, at one point or another, they can be broken. You do what is best to communicate what you need to. That's your priority — not adhering to rules.

FREEDOM RACEWAY is underlined. Any words you read on the screen: email, signs, sky-writing, Born To Lose tattoos, newspaper headlines, anything the audience reads should be underlined.

```
EXT. RACE TRACK — NIGHT

In front of a wildly CHEERING sell-out crowd,
two huge, lethal motorcycles — one black, one
red, side by side — race dangerously around the
oval and thunder for the finish line.
```

Rather than have one solid block of scene description, it's better to break it up and let your script page visually breathe with white space. The alternative is a solid,

somewhat daunting block of scene description. You want to make the experience of reading your script an easy one.

CHEERING is capitalized. All sounds are capitalized.

You should skip two lines before each new scene. Back in the day, screenwriters put a CUT TO: after every scene. That's old fashioned now, necessitating a double space between scenes for easy reading.

```
The Official waves his checked flag as the
black motorcycle just noses over the finish line
before the red.
```

Every time there's a slug line, there must be SCENE DESCRIPTION — that's the sentence with the Official.

```
EXT. — PIT AREA — NIGHT
DARREN, in skin-tight red leathers, a handsome,
buffed out blonde thirty years old, power slides
to a TIRE SCREECHING stop and jumps off the red
motorcycle.
```

Darren is the main character. It's best to physically describe the main characters so the reader can conjure up some visual image of him or her to help connect with them.

Notice DARREN is capitalized. All new characters who have dialogue have to be CAPITALIZED when we first see them.

TIRE SCREECHING — another capitalized sound.

```
                    DARREN
               (sarcastic)
          Real cute.
```

Every time a character speaks they get their own DIALOGUE BOX as shown above.

(SARCASTIC) Lots of screenwriters use parentheticals promiscuously. They should only be used when the dialogue could be misinterpreted without it. Darren could actually mean "Real cute." But, he means it sarcastically, therefore the use of the parentheticals.

(Jumping off his bike) is the way a lot of writers use parentheticals. It is wrong.

```
He whips off his helmet...

                    DARREN
                 (continued)
        Cheating scum!
```

When your character has two consecutive dialogue boxes, the second box must carry a (continued) or (CONT'D).

```
...and rushes BULLETS, six feet of evil in black
leather, who drops his black bike and heaves his
helmet at Darren.
```

You'll notice I broke up the action by using ellipses (...). That helps the flow of the action. Another thing to make the read a seductive one.

```
                    BULLETS
        Loser!
Bullets is thrown a tire iron from the crowd as
Darren runs toward him.

Darren stops and they face each other — the big
moment has arrived.
```

Notice I separated these two lines — as the first line is a shot of Bullet and the next a shot of Darren, rather than calling the shots, which directors hate, I get the same result without calling the shot.

Every scene must have its own arc of drama. Every scene must be fully realized. It must describe what is happening on the screen. Most scenes should have a beginning, middle, and end.

One of the truisms of screenwriting is CUT TO THE HEART OF THE SCENE.

The big moment has arrived.

An uncharacteristic-for-me novelistic touch. Should be used rarely — only when important or absolutely necessary to make a point — or not at all.

One of the keys to format is being consistent with your usage. The last thing you want the reader to be thinking about is how you formatted the script.

time clocks

A student was writing a big "run and jump" movie, which strangely ground to a halt on page seventy-two:

> **When in action/adventure movies do people take the time to eat in the cafeteria — then get undressed and get into bed to go to sleep? These people are in action. Keep them in action. Maybe you could create a little urgency in this by putting in a time clock to meet the deadline on about page forty.**
>
> **Think about compressing the timeline so it makes it much more dramatic and urgent. Lackadaisical is not a good place for this "run and jump" script to be.**

Time clocks — putting a deadline on the action — is a great way to create urgency in your script as well as functioning as a constant reminder to the reader/viewer where they are in the story.

A character racing for the deadline is a time-honored and very effective tool for you to use. (*Please see* URGENCY)

trailer scenes

I get to one of the big scenes in a script and the writer writes it minimally and moves on.

I contact him:

What's going on? This is a trailer scene. This is one of the scenes that is the essence of this movie. Write more description. Sell it.

    Rich drags Wally to safety.

This is one of the most visually exciting and dangerous scenes in the movie and you give it five words. It should be a full page, at least. The struggle, the danger, the near miss, just missing, two steps forward, three back; write. If you think it's too exciting — I'm kidding — you can always pull it back.

Frank Capra, one of the great storytellers of the 1930s and 1940s, said you need four great scenes to make a good movie. That was the old days. Now, I think, you need more like ten. I call them trailer scenes: the best of the movie, what you're selling, the scenes that appear in the trailer. It's what the studios look for to hook their marketing to. It's wise to identify those scenes for yourself and focus your rewriting on them so you can make sure those scenes reach their full potential.

You have to identify the big moments and sell them. You're not.

I'm feeling one of the big tasks for the rewrite will be isolating the big scenes and making them much more impactful.

transcending yourself

I was writing a movie of the week for CBS. John Frankenheimer — *The Manchurian Candidate* — was the director. Confronted by a major emotional crisis in the script, I wrote that the main character fell asleep. I thought it was an unusual twist.

At the network notes meeting, the executive in charge of the project, though generally liking the script, was flummoxed by my choice. "Our hero is sleeping? Sleeping!?!"

I smiled at him confidently, "I thought it was an interesting way for him to deal with the crisis." To prove my point, I continued, "And as a matter of fact, that's how *I* deal with big-deal crises. I fall right asleep."

There was deathly silence in the executive suites at CBS. The Executive was very gentle to me, a lot gentler than I deserved — and suggested I fix it in the rewrite. He said to give the character behavior that expresses his feelings. He can fight, scream, accuse, get physical, anything — as long as he does *something*.

In the rewrite, he threw a chair.

Everyone liked it.

That script, by the way, was never made. Not for reasons of my stunted emotionality, but more because of a screenwriting misstep.

I wrote in the script that to prove his absolute depravity, the bad guy kills the lead character's beloved horse. I didn't know the network executive was a dedicated horse owner himself. He was horrified. The picture never got made.

The lesson?

Don't have any of your characters kill a horse.

What I did learn was that *you can't write every character from your own experience.*

The trick is to transcend yourself — start looking at things the way you'd never dream of handling them.

I write very good female characters. I'm a relatively rough and tumble guy and people are always surprised I write so many sensitive female characters. Not only am I in touch with the feminine side of myself, I bring my masculinity to the female characters and it moves them a little off the mark, makes them more interesting than the run-of-the-mill stereotypical female character.

Stretch yourself. Try new things. Imagine yourself as someone else. We all have so many people inside us. Get in touch with all that. It's fun.

transitions

A very important part of screenwriting you don't learn from screenwriting books. It's what you learn in editing rooms trying to make films flow.

Moving from the last frame of a shot to the first frame of the incoming shot is the transition I'm talking about. How you go from shot to shot. It comes into play at the end of a scene and the transition to the next scene. I'm talking about the VISUAL TRANSITION.

You have a Melissa to Melissa cut. Same size images don't work in film. I believe the same subject matter cuts on paper also don't work. An intervening non-Melissa scene would solve that. And because we're talking about just words, Melissa and Melissa are the equivalent of same size images.

My theory is that readers of your script SEE the transitions, the cuts on some subliminal or subconscious level. So that bad cuts stop the flow and readability of your script. In the editing room, you quickly discover that similar images don't cut well — that different images do.

AN EXAMPLE

```
EXT. BACKYARD — DAY

The two dogs sniff around the pile of leaves.
Sitting in the sun reading his manuscript, Tom
is happy.
```

```
INT. KITCHEN — DAY

Tom fixes himself some chocolate ice cream.
```

It's a Tom to Tom cut. Not good.

The following is better.

```
EXT. BACKYARD — DAY

The two dogs sniff around the pile of leaves.
Sitting in the sun reading his manuscript, Tom
is happy.

EXT. KITCHEN — DAY

A dish of chocolate ice cream. Tom scoops
himself some into a dish.
```

A Tom to the intervening ice cream cut to the Tom cut. Better.

So when you're writing:

THE BEST CUTS are from a wide shot without calling it such — to a tight shot without labeling it. Or INT. to EXT.

If you cut from Character A to Character A — it's similar and therefore not so good.

If you cut from Character A to Character B back to Character A — that cut works because similar images are separated by an intervening image.

PRE-LAPPING SOUND

Another issue with transitions:

This is now the second SOUND from an incoming scene transition. My suggestion is — since no one really cares, and rightfully so, how the screenwriter would make the director's call of what shots to lead us in and out of the transition — don't do it.

In addition, it's a FALSE TRANSITION — meaning you don't have to write the transition so it works because the incoming sound — ON THE PAGE — always works

— but sometimes leaves directors with unworkable scene endings.

■ EXERCISE 16 — THE LAST WORD ON TRANSITIONS.

Do a TRANSITIONS READ on your script focusing on transitions and making each one flow.

three-act structure

(See RISING ACTION)

twists and turns

One of the issues I see most in reading screenplays is: the script sets up right away and announces what it is about. That's good. Unfortunately, most scripts make good on that and sure enough, it ends as you pretty much imagined it would. No twists. No turns. No surprises. No interest.

I wrote to a writer:

I think this works, though I think you should spend more time evolving the story — it's very simple, and the story plays out just as it seems it's going to. This is not a good thing. There needs to be more "stuff" going on — twists, turns, surprises, bigger scenes with more fun, and more, more, more.

Brainstorm more ideas — more things that could happen, more twists that will surprise the reader/viewer and send the script in ways that we didn't expect but work better than we expected. Get funnier — get more emotional — get more physical — push yourself.

Thinking counts as writing.

I think one of the solutions to this script is to expand and add wrinkles to Francine's arc. Where she's in control. It works for a while...then, it doesn't...she walks...she comes back...tries something else...it works, then doesn't...that type of thing. More!

Alexander Payne's *The Descendants* is a terrific film partly because the story keeps twisting and turning in unexpected ways. That was the pleasure in viewing it. I never knew where it was going. It presented itself simply going in one direction, then kept permutating and spinning in unexpected but logical ways.

Diablo Cody's *Young Adult* does the opposite. It presents itself as one story and ploddingly goes that way until it grinds to the end. It's not enough. I was twenty minutes ahead of the story all the way down the pike. After Cody's *Juno*, which I loved, this was a sorely disappointing effort by all involved except for Charlize Theron, who was terrific.

urgency

The screenwriter is writing an action script. Every word is important and she wrote:

```
They STROLL toward the elevator. They WALK to
the flight deck.
```

Hold on. How about adding some urgency? Rushing — give them something that needs attending as they talk, doors gliding open. Movement.

A student wrote:

TWO YEARS LATER

My comment was:

Two years later? There's no urgency when you tell a story with these kinds of time gaps. (*See* TIME CLOCKS)

You, as the writer, have to set the pace for your movie. If your characters relate to the action in a lackadaisical manner, your readers will do the same.

When the writer announces we've just jumped six months or a year or two years, it asks more questions. What happened? Nothing? What about the urgency of the story? What about the drama and the stakes? You mean we can delay the action two years? No big deal? I urge writers not to put in time gap titles. Just run the scenes. See how it plays.

vocabulary

The sheet her only raiment.

And for the people who don't know what that means?

She lifted the quellazaire.

Try not to use words that are unfamiliar to the reader — not in common usage — so the reader doesn't feel inadequate.

Subaltern?

Are you kidding me?

What I really wanted to say to those readers — I think we know each other well enough for me to be straight with you — was: the last thing you want is to make your reader feel stupid — at least stupider than you. I want to feel good reading your script. If you think you're impressing me with your esoteric vocabulary — you're not.

The Last Word on this: You make me feel stupid — I don't buy your script.

voice over

Screenwriters are forever feeling guilty and conflicted about voice over, that narrator or main character's voice that helps us through movies. With voice over we can hear the main character, a bunch of characters, or just an institutional narrative voice.

The conflict?

Should they use such a tried and true old chestnut like voice over?

Well, why not? It works.

The guilt?

It's so easy. They've seen it in so many great movies, but it's still way too easy.

The deal is it doesn't always work. Some writers use voice over as a storytelling crutch instead of writing scenes and end up *telling* the reader/viewer the movie rather than *showing* them.

If you are going to use voice over, you'd better bring something to it.

I recently was working on a writer's script and his voice over — it was a contemporary film noir script, where classically voice overs are used a lot — was just riffing and not tied to the images or the story. Didn't work.

He rewrote it and found that when we were enlightened by the voice over, or amused by it, it really worked well, brought a much richer voice to the character.

Notes to another writer highlighting what's bad about voice over:

I'm not convinced the ending is effective. The voice over distances us. It becomes a speech instead of a scene.

And to another writer:

The voice overs explaining the movie to us are not working. You should be leaving something for the reader/viewer to do. If you tell us everything, we're not going to pay attention. You have to make it work without the voice over.

And to another:

The voice over isn't giving us insights. It's stating the obvious or what we don't care about. Try it without and see how it works.

weighting your writing

FADE IN:
EXT. ESTATE — SUNSET
As the perfect orb of golden sunlight dips
below the jagged blackness of the treetops, a
burgundy Bentley with cream colored pin-striping
and gangster dark windows cruises silently up
the circuitous, tree-lined, one-lane bricked
driveway heading for, in the distance, a twenty-
seven room mansion, a classic Newport Grand
Dame, at the crest of a rise. Behind it, the
crashing surf pounds against the stormy bluffs.

EXT. MANSION — SUNSET
The Bentley stops without a sound. The front
driver's side door insinuates open — six-inch
stiletto heels CLACK CLACK CLACK against the
aged cobblestones as a pair of shapely legs
encased in the sheerest Parisian silk stockings
head quickly toward the mansion.

The legs belong to ALEXANDRA DeMORNAY, barely
twenty, with a body men have killed for and a
brain that usually is at least two steps ahead
of everyone in the room, is sheathed in a skin-
tight Chanel little black dress that accentuates
every one of her overflowing assets.

EXT. MANSION — FRONT DOOR — SUNSET
Alexandra moves past the erotic Greek sculpture
of a voluptuous woman being taken by ferocious
lions, then a sculpture of a woman being
consumed by the dancing fires of hell.

Alexandra flicks her silky blonde shoulder-length hair from in front of her eyes, but she's not smiling. Alexandra DeMornay is dead serious.

She stops in front of the front door, a solid oak plank that has to be ten foot high studded with gnarly bronze fixtures and heavy bars.

Alexandra's crimson polished fingernail reaches toward the buzzer and sensually presses it.

BING BONG BING BONG echoes through the cavernous innards of the mansion and Alexandra hears FOOTSTEPS getting louder. The door UNLOCKS WITH A GRINDING METALLIC SCRAPE and slowly swings open.

Standing there: LORD HAVENSWORTH FORTESQUE, fifties, distinguished, gray around the temples and regal-looking despite being as naked as the day he was born. It's not a pretty sight.

Alexandra looks him up and down, then with a voice as sweet as hemlock…

                    ALEXANDRA
          Just as I thought…

…and she pulls a pearl-handled, ornately engraved Derringer out of her beaded purse and BANG! BANG! BANG! BANG!

Four bullet holes appear almost magically in Lord Fortesque's chest and start bleeding.

                    LORD FORTESQUE
                 (in disbelief)
          You shot me!?

Alexandra smiles a lethal smile.

                    ALEXANDRA
          And I'm going to do it again.

BANG.

And Lord Fortesque collapses lifelessly to the herringbone-patterned parquet oak floor.

Okay, that's awful — way too dense, way too much detail. If you had to read a whole script like that it would be torture.

The issue?

WEIGHTING YOUR WRITING.

It's important.

As the screenwriter, you have to take responsibility for guiding the reader as to what is important, what they should pay attention to. You do that by changing your style of writing: *writing a lot of detail when it's important, and writing minimally when it's not.*

Above, how important to the Alexandra-plugging-Lord F-scene is the pattern of the oak parquet floor? How important is it that the floor is oak? How important is it to mention the floor at all.

We don't need to know that the driveway is circuitous, brick-lined and one-lane. We don't need to know that the cobblestones are aged; we don't need to know that there are cobblestones and we don't want to know.

The scene is about DeMornay killing Lord Fortesque — it's not really about the pearl-handled, ornately engraved Derringer or the erotic Greek sculpture of the voluptuous woman being consumed by the dancing fires of hell, or the cream colored pin-striping on the burgundy Bentley.

That kind of promiscuous writing exhausts readers. After reading endless, meaningless details with no story pay off, the reader learns not to trust you — and then, after a while, becomes fed up, puts your script down, cracks open a beer and watches the game.

All that wordy over-descriptive writing is just not needed and borders on the abusive. A bit of an overstatement, but you get the point.

Your job as screenwriter is to seduce the reader. You want to hook them in the first five pages, then keep ramping up the seduction so you hold them in your grip for a hundred and five pages without repeating yourself. The last thing you want to do is exhaust the reader and reading overwritten writing does that.

Here's the re-written scene:

```
FADE IN:

EXT. ESTATE — SUNSET

A burgundy Bentley cruises up the driveway
heading for the classic Newport mansion.

The Bentley stops and the driver's side door
opens.

Stiletto heels below a pair of shapely legs
head toward the front door. The legs belong to
ALEXANDRA DeMORNAY, barely twenty, sheathed in a
skin-tight black dress.

She presses the doorbell. CHIMES echo inside of
the mansion.

FOOTSTEPS approach, the door UNLOCKS and slowly
swings open. It's LORD FORTESQUE, fifties, a
distinguished, six-foot, very naked man.

Alexandra looks him up and down.

                    ALEXANDRA
          Just as I thought…

She pulls a pearl-handed Derringer out of her
pocket and BANG! BANG! BANG! BANG!

Four bullet holes pop on Lord Fortesque's chest.

                    LORD FORTESQUE
          You shot me!?

Alexandra smiles a lethal smile.

                    ALEXANDRA
          And I'm going to do it again.

BANG.

Lord Fortesque collapses lifelessly to the
floor.
```

The first, too long version: 401 words. The rewritten version: 142 words — around one third of the words and what did I lose? No content, just some self-indulgent style. So, pick your spots.

In the important parts of scenes — MORE IS MORE.
And in the less important passages — LESS IS MORE.

we see, we hear

Please don't use:

```
We see the car,
```

or

```
We hear the music,
```

or

```
We follow them down the hall.
```

The point is what else would be going on? We see everything on the screen. We don't need to tell the reader that we do. The same goes for sounds. We don't need to tell the reader that we hear people speaking or hear bells ringing. Ring the bell. We hear it. Talk. We hear it.

what do you
want us to feel?

One of the questions I ask screenwriters when I finish reading their scripts is "What do you want the reader to feel?" It's a vital question because the ending has to be satisfying — not happy or sad — but satisfying.

I had a screenwriter whose main character, someone we've been investing in for a hundred pages, right before the ending, is run over by a bus. No fault of his, just a random act. I asked him what he wants the reader to feel other than hatred for the screenwriter?

The ending should make sense with the body of the script. It should be an outgrowth of the behavior and incidents in the script. It's great when the ending is a surprise, but makes all the sense in the world.

Think about the feelings of your reader. They're investing their time and hopefully their money in your characters, in their journey. You want it to pay off in a satisfying way for them. When writers write ambiguous, I'll-let-the-reader-decide-what-the-ending-is, I think it makes the ending less than satisfying.

When I read scripts where everything is going along fine, then the main character at the end puts a .357 Magnum into his mouth and blows his head off, I always wonder what the writer wants the reader/viewer to feel?

Part of the deal we writers have with reader/viewers is how we pay off our scripts. Make sure you leave the reader/viewer the way you want to.

what hooks them?

Notes to a writer about what makes readers stay with their script:

About now I'm feeling a little overloaded with information and history and politics and need some emotional tie into this piece.

Information isn't enough — we access the script through the humanity.

Bring the human story up and the political story back. I'm looking for a better, more emotionally satisfying balance.

what should you be writing about?

You should be writing about what you care about.

You should be writing something you'd want to see.

You should be writing about something that fascinates you.

You should be writing something you know.

You should write the movie that's going to make you a fortune.

You should write something that scares you.

You should write the script you don't think you're a good enough writer to write.

You should write something you believe in.

You should write a script that deals with emotions you're afraid to face.

what we write
movies about

Notes to screenwriters about what they're writing about:

**This script is beginning to feel that it's undeveloped
— not the writing — the story, and the ambitions of
the script. You've set the bar too low. You need more.
Lots more.**

And to another writer:

**I think one of the issues in this script is you're trying to
do too much.**

**It always concerns me when writers want to go beyond
entertaining to educate — this might not be the venue
for that. Stay focused on your 'A' story.**

And another:

**There's something wrong here: everybody is sitting
around doing drug raps. Who cares? I think you have
to earn it. The ideas are progressing but the story isn't.
And the characters aren't evolving. We're just doing the
same thing over and over again — taking drugs and riffing. Not enough.**

And to this writer:

**I'm thirty-seven pages in. The script has been predomi-
nately two people talking in a room. Not doing anything,
just talking. Not enough movement. Not enough behavior. Not enough movie. Not enough evolution of story.**

Not enough. Why is this a movie? Simply put, at the
moment it's not.

And this one:

Every time I read about Sam's dream to open a tamale
shop in Texas, I wonder what would happen if his dream
— which drives the whole movie and unfortunately
barely plays at the end — was sexier — like a motorcycle shop or a bar, or whatever? Something bigger
maybe or more dangerous, more of a dreamer, more of
the cinematic elements we want to make movies about.
I think the whole story has to be cranked up so that it's
movie-worthy.

Here's another one:

Your script feels like it needs to be opened up. Now, it's
a doper/video straight to DVD, you direct. But if you're
looking to sell this — think about opening it up and
getting much trippier. After all, it is a doper movie.

And another:

I'm getting a feeling that one of the big issues of this
screenplay is that you're thinking about these scenes
as springboards for ideas, aging riffs, your observations
about growing old, rather than thinking of these scenes
as reporting on behavior, movement, actions.

Another:

Movies — MOTION PICTURES — are about movement,
about watching things take place and evolve and, in the
best of movies, we're left to our own devices in terms
of what things mean. We watch and put it together. This
script has none of that. We listen to this script. There's
not much to watch.

And finally:

This is a five or so page scene with two people sitting
and talking. Think about moving it to Central Park,
walking the paths, seeing the sights, being interrupted,

being sold drugs, roller skaters, runners, dogs, people they know versus sitting for five minutes and talking. It's five percent of your movie. And before this, the dinner party is also just sitting and talking.

Nope, one more:

If I were a doper and could teleport and dope was uppermost in my head, I'd TP to Amsterdam for a toke — maybe Morocco for some hash. I'd trip to the Northern Lights for a light show. I'd go into DEA, 'cause they'd have the best dope. Then, I'd try NIMH for some acid, then I'd want to answer some questions: gold in Fort Knox? Scarlett Johansson naked? Aliens at Area 51? That's what we make movies about, versus going to Cindy Lou's apartment and hiding behind the curtain. This is a movie idea — write it.

writer's block

Well, here's the thing: I'm not a big believer in Writer's Block.

Sure I get it that writing a screenplay doesn't always come easy. But writers not writing because they lack the inspiration — well, spare me. My job is to be a writer and if I don't write — I don't have food on my table. I have to write. It's my job. Inspiration is fine. Working is better. I'm a writer.

If I don't feel inspired to solve a particular scene and feel stuck, I'll go back and rewrite yesterday's work, or I'll skip over the unsolved scene I'm not inspired to fix and move to the next one. The idea is keep writing, keep moving forward, keep at it. Show up as a writer every day and write.

In my present on-site class, a writer hadn't had the inspiration to come up with the story yet, and was struggling.

I told him to write character biographies and, as expected, the process of doing that "inspired" a story. Writing begets writing. The more you write the better you get.

Don't give into writer's block. It's like people who procrastinate and do the laundry or anything before writing. That's bullshit. You want to be a writer. Write. Don't be so easy on yourself.

writer's mantra

I'm doing a private consultation and the writer emailed:

"Hey, Tom —
I'm having trouble writing. It's like I have anxiety when
I get to my computer. It's like how real is it that I have a
chance to make a living out there as a screenwriter? So I
start thinking about that and end up not writing."

I hear you, Laurie, I really do. The reality is you have as much a chance as anyone else to make it as a screenwriter. It's a long shot for everyone. With all the film schools and interest in film, there are a lot scripts and a lot of screenwriters. That's the reality. You can't let it freak you out.

One of the things that has kept me alive and writing is the belief I have always had: that good scripts will ultimately surface and be noticed.

I've written something like fifty original scripts. Of those, I always felt that four of them were going to be made. Three of them have been made and the fourth is being read by a production company. Laurie, I do believe if you write a great script, it will be noticed.

I also want to address what's going on in your head. That may not be the usual agenda for a script consultation, but it's important.

Many writers I've come across have a particularly negative mantra going through their mind — something like: "Who's going to read this? I can't do this. This stinks. Why would anyone read this, no less buy it? I'm wasting my time. I'm a loser." This is not a positive thing and it affects the writer's enjoyment of writing. It's a problem.

I'm lucky. My natural writer's mantra goes something like this: "I'd like to thank the Academy of Motion Picture Arts and Sciences for this well-deserved Oscar for Original Screenplay. I'm accepting this award for screenwriters everywhere."

My advice is try to turn your mantra around — change the tape in your head to a positive one — it might make your writing experience more pleasurable.

■ EXERCISE 17 – THE LAST WORD ON MANTRAS.

Write a short, positive mantra that you put into your head every time your negative tape starts playing.

writing a page-turner

I think every screenwriter hopes they can write a script that once a reader picks it up, they will not be able to put it down. That's the definition of a page-turner.

How do you write a page-turner?

A couple of ways.

Of course, there's RISING ACTION — constantly upping of the stakes in your story that we've dealt with previously.

The second major way to write a page-turner is to **control the dissemination of the information**.

The idea is to keep NEW INFORMATION flowing to the reader while ALWAYS PROMISING THEM MORE.

That's the formula — doling out information on a regular basis, always giving the reader some new story element every four or five pages and at the same time teasing them about the exciting information yet to come. You always want the reader to want to turn the page to find out what's going to happen.

So, giving the reader a constant, evolving flow of new information and constantly raising the stakes will make your script a page-turner.

Focusing on ARCING your writing is another way to get readers turning the page. If all your characters are changing, not behaving the same from scene to scene; in other words, if your characters are evolving, your reader/viewer gets caught in the momentum of the characters' journey.

SURPRISES are another way to tantalize the reader to keep reading. The less you set up, so that the reader/viewer doesn't know what's coming, the more the reader will be encouraged to turn the page.

TWISTS, TURNS, and WRINKLES add a great deal to your storytelling. I've mentioned this before. While you are arcing everything — that arc doesn't necessarily have to be a smooth arc — it can always keep its upward direction, but have changes of pace — small downs or valleys on the steady trail up.

RHYTHM and MOMENTUM are two techniques you should think about in designing your script. As you get closer and closer to the end of your script, it's a good idea to increase the speed of the film, meaning: shorter scenes, quicker dialogue, a faster pace of storytelling.

Employing some or all of the above will go a long way to making your script A PAGE-TURNER.

wrong words

In this world of Spell Check and lesser quality educations, the use of wrong words seems to be epidemic. Or, I've become more intolerant. In any event, here are some of the ones I've come across in the last few years.

Beyond just amusing you, I'd like to see you go through your script and make sure you're not using any wrong words.

SOME OF MY FAVORITES:
> It was an impressive feet.
> She stood no more then three feat a way.
> That's for shore.
> I was on a role.
> I was cast in the roll of Pedro.
> He opens the vile and pours out the poison.
> I think he's vial.
> I gauze into her eyes.
> She wrapped his wound in gaze.
> I could feel it in my crouch.
> She crotched down to see.
> I could see her face pail.
> I filled the pale with sand.
> I feel feint.
> He fainted left and went right.
> Comedy is one of the stables of TV. (A favorite)
> I was entering the very vowels of hell.
> I jammed on the breaks.
> They'll brake into the joint.
> He's hiding in the chicken coup.

Smashed potatoes.
He waved the clause.
She walks passed him.
There's the ally cat.
He was going to the bowls of hell.
He's a nuclear physic.
He went trough.
General Patent climbs out of the Gyp. (A twofer.)
A siren whales in the street.
He ducts and the ball flies over him.
She stables the papers together.
He looses his cool.
She complements him.
He was good at razing capitol. (Another twofer.)
She kicked the tenet out.
She ran into the Nevada dessert.
Died blonde hare.
He lost his composer. (My all-time favorite)
He hugged her around the waste.
They're/there/their. (Take your pick)
He challenges the Count to a dual.
You're, yore, your. (Take your pick)
He opened the box and walah. (*Voila!* — another favorite!)
He couldn't hear. He was def.
Candid yams.
Peace of paper.
She joined the click.
He stairs him down.
It was her soul responsibility.
He checks his wait on the scale.
Bagel and locks.
He jumps from the plane and his shoot opens.
The game is whining down.
Piqué/peak/peek. (Take your pick)
She was a randy winch.
It's the other won.

postscript

I'd like to thank all the writers and students who donated their snippets of notes and writing. In each case, the writing was dramatically reconfigured — changing all character names, situations, locations, subject matter to ensure the integrity of their scripts. Everyone's ideas are safe. No secrets have been revealed, no confidences betrayed.

Pundits and media gurus are forever trying to predict the future of the movie business and television and where we're going media-wise. I think we all have to pay attention to that.

Accordingly, I've stopped thinking of myself as a screenwriter. I'm really a storyteller, as you are. That's what we do. That's our talent, or our gift, or our curse, depending how you look at it.

Wherever the future takes us, my guess is they're always going to need storytellers.

The Last Word is: Your name goes on the script and you have to take the ultimate responsibility for how it's written. If you apply the information in this book, your story and characters will be given the cleanest framework they can be given so the reader can fully engage in exactly what you want them to engage in.

And remember, if after reading the book you're stuck, email me at LAZARUSTOM@AOL.COM with your question and I'll answer it.

Keep writing, and keep thinking about writing.

tom lazarus —
script consultant

I work with screenwriters around the world at every level —
beginners to pros — to raise the level of their writing and of the
script they're writing.

I teach using the more contemporary structure motifs and
work on script from inception to the submission drafts.

I evaluate the screenwriter's needs and custom design a
course of instruction that will help the screenwriter accomplish
his or her goals.

If you'd like more information on a script consultation, email
me at LAZARUSTOM@AOL.COM.

about the author

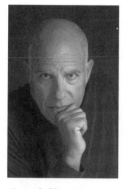

After training to be an artist, Tom Lazarus' first career was in entertainment advertising, where he created campaigns for the major motion picture studios. He also designed album covers and was nominated for a Grammy.

His second career was writing, directing, and producing educational and business films. He won more than two dozen international film festival honors including Best Educational Film of the Year at the San Francisco Film Festival. He was nominated for a CLIO for directing a Fair Housing Public Service TV spot.

Then, Tom started writing for television, writing seven Movies of the Week for the networks including *Mazes and Monsters* with Tom Hanks, *The Ordeal of Bill Carney*, and *The Brainwashing of Canda Torres*, and working as a staff writer/ story editor for nine network series, including *Hunter*, *Jake and the Fatman*, *Starman*, *Stingray*, *Mike Hammer*, and *War of the Worlds*.

His feature credits include the original story for the George Burns/Brooke Shields motion picture *Just You and Me, Kid*, the script for the Swedish-made *Revenge and Justice*, and the #1 film in America upon its release, *Stigmata*. He has had nine feature films made from his original screenplays.

Tom has directed five feature films: *Movies Kill*, *Word of Mouth*, *House of Love*, *Voyeur Confessions*, and *Exhibitionist Files*.

He wrote, directed and executive produced five seasons of the cable TV hit *7 Lives Xposed*.

He has published two books through St. Martin's Press, *Secrets of Film Writing* and *Rewriting Secrets for Screenwriters*.

Presently Tom is teaching The Master Class in Screenwriting and the online Screenwriting Mentorship Program at UCLA Extension, Writers Program.

He has also taught undergraduate screenwriting at the University of California Santa Barbara and a Master Class at California State University Northridge.

Recently, Tom wrote and directed the sold-out theatre piece *Stevie Stern as Jewel Parker* at the Hudson Theater in Los Angeles, and has just sent out his new screenplay, *Hollywood Capone*.

Tom Lazarus lives in Los Angeles with his wife, writer/actress Stevie, and the two sweetest terrier-adjacent dogs in the world, Ike and Bella Luna.

SAVE THE CAT!®
THE LAST BOOK ON SCREENWRITING YOU'LL EVER NEED!

BLAKE SNYDER

BEST SELLER

He's made millions of dollars selling screenplays to Hollywood and now screenwriter Blake Snyder tells all. "Save the Cat!®" is just one of Snyder's many ironclad rules for making your ideas more marketable and your script more satisfying — and saleable, including:

- The four elements of every winning logline.
- The seven immutable laws of screenplay physics.
- The 10 genres and why they're important to your movie.
- Why your Hero must serve your idea.
- Mastering the Beats.
- Mastering the Board to create the Perfect Beast.
- How to get back on track with ironclad and proven rules for script repair.

This ultimate insider's guide reveals the secrets that none dare admit, told by a show biz veteran who's proven that you can sell your script if you can save the cat.

"Imagine what would happen in a town where more writers approached screenwriting the way Blake suggests? My weekend read would dramatically improve, both in sellable/producible content and in discovering new writers who understand the craft of storytelling and can be hired on assignment for ideas we already have in house."
> – From the Foreword by Sheila Hanahan Taylor, Vice President, Development at Zide/Perry Entertainment, whose films include *American Pie, Cats and Dogs, Final Destination*

"One of the most comprehensive and insightful how-to's out there. Save the Cat!® is a must-read for both the novice and the professional screenwriter."
> – Todd Black, Producer, *The Pursuit of Happyness, The Weather Man, S.W.A.T, Alex and Emma, Antwone Fisher*

"Want to know how to be a successful writer in Hollywood? The answers are here. Blake Snyder has written an insider's book that's informative — and funny, too."
> – David Hoberman, Producer, *The Shaggy Dog* (2005), *Raising Helen, Walking Tall, Bringing Down the House, Monk* (TV)

BLAKE SNYDER, besides selling million-dollar scripts to both Disney and Spielberg, was one of Hollywood's most successful spec screenwriters. Blake's vision continues on *www.blakesnyder.com*.

$19.95 · 216 PAGES · ORDER NUMBER 34RLS · ISBN: 9781932907001

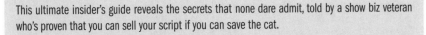

24 HOURS | **1.800.833.5738** | **WWW.MWP.COM**

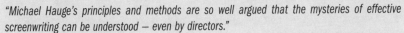

THE SCRIPT-SELLNG GAME - 2ND ED.
A HOLLYWOOD INSIDER'S LOOK AT GETTING YOUR SCRIPT SOLD AND PRODUCED

KATHIE FONG YONEDA

The Script-Selling Game is about what they never taught you in film school. This is a look at screenwriting from the other side of the desk — from a buyer who wants to give writers the guidance and advice that will help them to not only elevate their craft but to also provide them with the down-in-the-trenches information of what is expected of them in the script selling marketplace.

It's like having a mentor in the business who answers your questions and provides you with not only valuable information, but real-life examples on how to maneuver your way through the Hollywood labyrinth. While the first edition focused mostly on film and television movies, the second edition includes a new chapter on animation and another on utilizing the Internet to market yourself and find new opportunities, plus an expansive section on submitting for television and cable.

"I've been writing screenplays for over 20 years. I thought I knew it all — until I read The Script-Selling Game. *The information in Kathie Fong Yoneda's fluid and fun book really enlightened me. It's an invaluable resource for any serious screenwriter."*

> — Michael Ajakwe Jr., Emmy-winning TV producer, *Talk Soup*; Executive Director of Los Angeles Web Series Festival (LAWEBFEST); and creator/ writer/director of *Who...* and *Africabby* (AjakweTV.com)

"Kathie Fong Yoneda knows the business of show from every angle and she generously shares her truly comprehensive knowledge — her chapter on the Web and new media is what people need to know! She speaks with the authority of one who's been there, done that, and gone on to put it all down on paper. A true insider's view."

> — Ellen Sandler, former co-executive producer of *Everybody Loves Raymond* and author of *The TV Writer's Workbook*

KATHIE FONG YONEDA has worked in film and television for more than 30 years. She has held executive positions at Disney, Touchstone, Disney TV Animation, Paramount Pictures Television, and Island Pictures, specializing in development and story analysis of both live-action and animation projects. Kathie is an internationally known seminar leader on screenwriting and development and has conducted workshops in France, Germany, Austria, Spain, Ireland, Great Britain, Australia, Indonesia, Thailand, Singapore, and throughout the U.S. and Canada.

$19.95 · 248 PAGES · ORDER NUMBER 161RLS · ISBN 13: 9781932907919

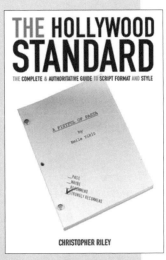

{ THE MYTH OF MWP }

In a dark time, a light bringer came along, leading the curious and the frustrated to clarity and empowerment. It took the well-guarded secrets out of the hands of the few and made them available to all. It spread a spirit of openness and creative freedom, and built a storehouse of knowledge dedicated to the betterment of the arts.

The essence of the Michael Wiese Productions (MWP) is empowering people who have the burning desire to express themselves creatively. We help them realize their dreams by putting the tools in their hands. We demystify the sometimes secretive worlds of screenwriting, directing, acting, producing, film financing, and other media crafts.

By doing so, we hope to bring forth a realization of 'conscious media' which we define as being positively charged, emphasizing hope and affirming positive values like trust, cooperation, self-empowerment, freedom, and love. Grounded in the deep roots of myth, it aims to be healing both for those who make the art and those who encounter it. It hopes to be transformative for people, opening doors to new possibilities and pulling back veils to reveal hidden worlds.

MWP has built a storehouse of knowledge unequaled in the world, for no other publisher has so many titles on the media arts. Please visit www.mwp.com where you will find many free resources and a 25% discount on our books. Sign up and become part of the wider creative community!

Onward and upward,

Michael Wiese
Publisher/Filmmaker